# FOUR SQUARE

| | |
|---|---|
| 1 | 2 |
| 3 | 4 |

# SELLING

## Allen Carmichael

CONCEPT

By the same author:
**"MULTI-LEVEL MARKETING"**
ISBN 1 873288 00 X
*Concept* - July 1990

2nd Edition - retitled **"NETWORK & MULTI-LEVEL MARKETING"**
ISBN 1 873288 01 8
*Concept*  - September 1991
Reprinted - June 1993
            April 1994 (with additions)

**"THE NETWORK MARKETING SELF-STARTER"**
ISBN 1 873288 02 6
*Concept* - November  1991

**"BELIEVE YOU CAN!"**
ISBN 1 873288 03 4
*Concept* November 1992

ISBN 1 873288 04 2
Book and cover design by Allen Carmichael
Printed in Finland by Werner Söderström Osakeyhtiö

# Contents

*"Everyone lives by selling something"*

**Robert Louis Stevenson 1850-1894**

# *Introduction*

From a behavioural point of view, all of life is a game - and all games are, or should be, played according to a set of rules.

The way we react to one another, the thrust and response of all human contact, is played out by the participants on a continuing basis, but often, unfortunately, with only scant knowledge of, or a complete disregard for the ground rules. That is why so many relationships break down and so many potentially rewarding experiences are frustrated - and why so many sales are lost!

People's relationships fail when they stop selling to one another. In our everyday lives all too often we behave badly, unthinkingly, and without sufficient consideration one for the other. It is too easy to say things in a fleeting moment, expressing anger, frustration, irritation - feelings and emotional thrusts that can never be retrieved - or at best may take days, weeks, even years to repair.

We spend our lives, so far as personal relationships go, forever repairing fences, trying to redress delicate balances upset or disturbed as a result of ill-considered words and actions that, with a little more thought and consideration as well as a greater awareness of the rules of the game, might have been averted.

## SELLING MIRRORS LIFE
Selling has been described as *the greatest game of all.* It is based very much on what I call *the rules of engagement.* A series of unwritten edicts must be observed, if the intended outcome - a sale - is to take place - or, indeed, looked at from the other person's side of the fence, be averted!

1

A sale, just like any personal relationship - is a fragile and transient thing, easily damaged, sometimes utterly shattered, destroyed by an unthinking action or ill-considered word. In the context of the sales situation, there must always be an awareness of feelings, the temperature of the water, awareness of empathy - or lack of it - and, in fact, an awareness of all the subtleties of innuendo that go to make up any relationship. In selling, though not always in life, we are more likely to play the game by the rules simply because there is something measurable at stake - *our income!* But it seems to me that selling is what life itself is about, so once one has mastered the art of selling, all the acquired knowledge and understanding could be applied to almost everything we do in the greater sphere of life.

As I have suggested, *selling is not just for sales people.* Having said that, the thought suggests itself that, in fact, we are *all* sales people. The politician on the hustings is only selling himself and his party to the voters, and once elected, he continues the selling process in putting across his ideas and political policies. All too often his words fall on deaf ears simply because he *tells* rather than *sells.*

Governments spend tens of millions of pounds each year on screening people for the possibility of impending coronary heart disease whilst advising them to either stop smoking or to lose weight. This expenditure, in the case of this country, has rarely been demonstrated to have had any significant effect on the statistics related to these causes. That suggests to me that something doesn't work, wouldn't you agree - despite the astronomic amount being expended? The simple truth is that *people do not like to be lectured* - and that, I would suspect is exactly what is happening, and why the results are not justifying the amount of money being thrown at the exercise. The concept of not smoking or of losing weight cannot be put across by simply telling people about the dangers involved. My last book ('*Believe you can!*') was devoted to the idea that anyone can achieve anything in life. In writing this introduction, I realise that that last book was really on *selling!* It was concerned with the one simple precept that ***desire is the starting point for all change.***

If one wants change, and the desire is great enough, there is nothing to stop that change coming about. Going back to the heart disease statistics, the approach should be to get people to *feel* something about the fact they smoke or *feel* something about the fact they are over weight. If asked the simple question, '*do you want to give up smoking?*', the majority of smokers will answer YES, even though they are doing nothing about it - and that YES is the *very first step* towards creating the *desire* to stop. Similarly, if asked the simple question, '*do you think you would feel better if you weighed less?*', the majority of obese people will also answer YES. They may, at that point, have no intention whatsoever of doing anything about it, but again, that YES represents a starting point towards *selling* the idea rather than merely delivering a reprimanding lecture that does no more than produce a feeling of stubborn antagonism.

It would not be untrue to say that people who are generally successful, both in life and business, are good at selling. They have acquired a real understanding of the rules that govern the game.

**Living life successfully *is* selling!**

Unfortunately, it would not be true to suggest that success in selling is necessarily the gateway to successful living. I would very much like to think that if selling is conducted on the basis of the *Four-Square* principle, a beneficial effect would be bound to spill over into an individual's general life style. After all, just as much is at stake in life as in any sales situation.

Some years ago I met a man who was both a powerful preacher in the religious sect of which he was the leader, as well as being a wealthy man through his business which was concerned with building and property development. He proudly told me how he had made a lot of money by taking advantage of a customer in a particular set of circumstances. Being somewhat taken aback by this statement, I asked him how he could reconcile that sort of business behaviour with his religious beliefs. He looked at me with undisguised astonishment and replied simply, *'what has business to do with religion?'*

## THE SALESMAN'S STATUS
Unfortunately in this country we have in the past - almost, it would seem, by tradition - given the occupation of selling a status that put it very near the bottom of the socio-economic scale. The salesman, for example, has always been placed very near the end of the risk league table used by insurance companies, grouped with actors and artists as being regarded as unreliable, and therefore a poor risk.

In the United States of America the salesman has always been accorded both status and dignity and is regarded as a professional, not merely a person doing a job. Happily though, in Britain, attitudes have moved through something of a change over the past couple of decades and salespeople do now enjoy a rather better place in society - but, nevertheless, are still regarded with an almost traditional distrust.

Salesmen are perceived to have real value as both company assets and as assets to our national economy. We in Britain are inclined to look at American methods of selling as "a bit over the top" - what we perhaps don't always take into account is that they fit the context and style of American life in a way that doesn't always work here. We may have taken certain fast food brand names to our hearts, but we still retain a small, nagging suspicion of many American attitudes. As an island race we have maintained - and not always to our credit - an insularity in our acceptance of ideas from outside. Why else would we constantly kick against and disagree with many E.E.C. rulings?

## SELLING IS NEGOTIATING

This book has been written to put forward a concept of sales behaviour that could be followed anywhere in the world. Selling, when all is said and done, is no more than negotiating - and negotiating is just an inter-play between people and attitudes, involving every aspect of normal human behaviour.

Sales training in Britain has developed and evolved considerably over the past decade or so, and advances in technology have played no small part in aiding both the sales process and the training of sales people. Audio tapes, videos and seminars all have their place in the scheme of things, as does CBT (Computer Based Training). But we must be on our guard and never allow computer technology to carry us too far away from the *reality* of the sales process - ***the vitally important relationship between salesman and customer.***

5

Selling comes down to *two human beings playing the games people play!* Nothing, but nothing, can replace the sheer emotional power of human relationships.

The amateur, in almost any field of human endeavour, is usually frustrated by the technicalities surrounding whatever he or she is hoping to achieve. It is the constant and annoying awareness of not being sufficiently skilled in the use of tools, materials and disciplines which is a stumbling block to the immediate achievement of a totally satisfying outcome.

The problem can only be solved through sheer activity on the basis that the more work one does, the more skilled one will become in the use of the elements required, until any perceived barrier has been removed. When this occurs - the point at which one does not have to constantly think *'how do I do this?'* - one can begin to pose the question *'why do I want to do this?'* And that is the point at which real creativity, regardless of the area of activity, can emerge. It is creativity that enhances all human activity, all human life, providing flexibility, originality, and a greater interest in and awareness of potential.

True creativity has no boundaries. Georges Braques used to say that if one could visualise a painting so clearly that all one had to do was paint it, the result would be worthless as it would be untouched by the spirit of creativity. Creativity is exploiting the accidental and always being sufficiently flexible and open-minded to recognise the value of an accident when it occurs. But, at that point, *the inability to handle both tools and materials expertly could be the stumbling block.* The whole process only comes together when whatever one wishes to do can be done quite unconsciously - without reference to the *how?* question. In the case of painting, what the mind conceives can be translated straight onto the canvas without any conscious thought. The only question of constant and real significance is *'why?'*

That process, when it is achieved, represents complete mastery of both equipment and tools so that no barrier exists between the mind and the physical transformation of ephemeral ideas into a visible and tangible form.

It is these thoughts that lie behind the four-square principle of selling - the notion of dealing with the immediate problem without constantly worrying about the outcome. In golf, it is concentrating one's entire attention on the ball at one's feet, and on what must be done with that, rather than being preoccupied with *where* it is going. Solve the immediate problem and the long-term solution - where the ball will land - will take care of itself.

Selling can teach us *control* and a greater understanding of the complexity of relationships. There is a great deal to learn both about life and about selling and if increased knowledge of either can be instrumental in the improvement of both, the outcome can be nothing but beneficial. This, I hasten to add, is in no way an evangelistic view! All I want to do at this point is to sow the small seed of an idea in your mind before you get into the real substance of this book. Judge for yourself when you emerge at the other end...

**NOTE:** You will no doubt have noticed in this introduction, the constant use of the word *salesman*. I will continue throughout the book to use the word *salesman* and employ *him* and *his* as the words to refer to the person engaged in the selling profession. I considered at length the use of words such as *sales person* and the constant use of devices such as *his/her*, but these things seem rather pedantic and would, I am sure, become very boring to the reader.

By the use of the masculine throughout the book, the last thing I would wish to do is to offend any female readers - so may I simply say, for *salesman*, please read *sales woman*, or even *sales person*, if that should be your preference. The word is employed merely as a useful device to make reading the book easier.

*Allen Carmichael - August 1994*

# SECTION 1

## *<u>The Sales Philosophy</u>*
### *<u>&</u>*
## *<u>FOUR-SQUARE-SELLING</u>*

# 1
# *Getting to grips with the situation*

It has often been said that the reason so many people didn't get off the *Titanic* was simply that they didn't know what was happening...

In another of my books I mentioned a report of some years ago concerning a questionnaire that had been sent to 2000 people in the United States. The thing these people had in common was that they had all "failed" in the Life Assurance industry - an industry very much concerned with direct selling. The idea behind this project was to try to discover whether there was some common denominator that might account for this apparently wanton waste of human resources. The answer that eventually emerged as the only common factor was a very simple one indeed - *'nobody told me what to do'*.

## SELLING - A DEFINITION
Selling is *bringing value to the person who is buying.*

## Telling is *not* selling!

People hate to be *sold* something - but they love to *buy* something, for by so doing, *they* are making the decision.

## Buying is fun!

People buy what a product or service *can do for them,* rather than buying that product or service for its apparent face value.

They buy because it makes them *feel good.* It produces what we could call the feel-good-factor, and that is something everyone enjoys.

The ability to sell is one of man's natural accomplishments. Because he is a naturally emotional creature he feels enthusiasm and derives enjoyment from sharing the objects of his enthusiasm. *Selling* at its very best is *sharing,* but the act of selling has become confused through too much importance being placed on *how* it should be done. Teaching has produced barriers and barriers so often create apprehension, anxiety and even fear. The emotion most disliked by a human being is that of being rejected. That old bogey man, *fear of rejection,* is what so much of this book is about. It is also very much concerned with another phenomenon - an anxiety so many would-be salesmen experience - *anxiety over closing a sale.*

## THE *WHY* AND *HOW* ROUTES

The answer to so much in life lies in these two simple and apparently innocent little words. When faced with a problem, imagine yourself travelling along a road and coming upon a fork with a signpost. One arm of the signpost says WHY and the other bears the word HOW. Which direction would you instinctively take?

*Why* is often related to desire. Supposing you were faced with learning a language. The task looks fairly daunting when you pose the question *how do I start?* - or *how* will I ever manage to learn so much?

But ask yourself the question *why?* - *why* am I going to learn this language? The answer might simply be because you like the idea of being able to speak that language as it could bring added value to holidays or your business. There

**12**

could be all manner of reasons but they will all relate to *desire* in one way or another. *Every attempt at change starts with desire for that change.* It is desire that will produce the motivation to fire most achievement because if desire is driving you (i.e.*why), **how** the task will be accomplished will fall into place quite naturally.

If selling is approached by the *why* route, rather than the *how* route, and we remain aware that the aim of selling is to create good feelings of warmth and satisfaction - making the buyer feel good about himself and what he has done - it becomes very easy indeed.

## 3% OF THE POPULATION

Only recently someone told me how sad they felt many salesmen seemed to be. They are people, my informant claimed, often trapped in the selling situation simply because they must have a job. It has been suggested that the concept of selling only appeals to a mere handful of our population - something in the region of 3% - and yet I feel sure that a far greater proportion is actually engaged in the activity in one way or another. Many people do not like the image of the salesman and have no wish to be associated with the occupation for that reason. This is probably because there have usually been more bad salesmen about than good ones.

Would it therefore be fair to assume that if a great many people in sales don't actually like what they do, it might be because they don't know sufficient about it to make the job enjoyable? It might of course also be that they too do not like the image that appears to traditionally surround the business of selling. *Or perhaps nobody told them what to do - or what fun selling can be.*

Perhaps nobody pointed out to them that selling should produce good feelings in both the seller and the buyer or that

13

the seller's aim should be to bring added value to the buyer's life and the event should bring deep satisfaction to both sides.

## THE JOY OF BUYING!

Buying is said by psychologists to provide emotional release. It can bring out the child in us and recreate the excitement of the acquisition of a new toy!

The ultimate aim of a sale ought, as we have seen, to be to provide the buyer with a good feeling - the warm cosy glow of satisfaction that comes after doing something you wanted to do. Selling should be looked on as helping people to get what they want - what they desire. Once you come to the realisation that you are actually turned on by helping others to make decisions that make them feel good, you will have become more successful, acquired more friends and brought added value to a lot of people's lives.

Another thought on which to speculate is that the bad salesman just does not have sufficient interest in people to make his job the fascinating thing it could be. His attitude will be reflected in his pay packet. In most jobs you are paid what the job is worth - you are trading your time and freedom for money.

*In direct selling* ***you are paid what you are worth.***

You use time the way you want to in the creation of your own freedom.

I felt that a book which not only told aspiring salesmen what to do but also how to do it - and how to play the game by the rules - might achieve four things:

1. It could add to their enjoyment and make their working life more acceptable - if not actually fun!
2. It could make them better salesmen.
   This would be to their own advantage, as well as that of their customers and their employers.
3. It might be instrumental in helping them to play the greater game - life itself!
4. ...and it might be instrumental in adding considerably to their earnings!

## SELLING vs. ORDER-TAKING

Almost every company with a product or service to sell, offers its entrants - aspiring salesmen - technical training. This is often of a very high standard, but, as with all things in life, there are companies whose training falls far below any acceptable level. All too often, if an applicant has already been in selling in any of its many forms, it is assumed they already know all about it. Unfortunately also, in many instances, it is assumed that to give a trainee a smattering of knowledge about the company's products, they are thereby equipped to go forth and not only represent that company but present themselves as experts offering valuable and accurate advice. Selling, after all is only a matter of *telling the customer about the product*. We would of course all agree with that, wouldn't we? No? Well, lets take a look at that statement.

There is a very big difference between selling and order-taking. There are many people who are perfectly capable of maintaining cosy established relationships with customers, appearing at predictable intervals to check on stock and take an order that, in reality, could just as easily have been posted or dealt with by telephone or fax. The reason for employing an order-taker is that, in all probability, that order would not have been posted, telephoned or faxed at that particular time, such is the way of the world and the way things happen - *or don't!*

But really there is more to it than that. Maintaining personal contact has great value, and the employer may regard the salary of his order-taker amply justified as a public relations exercise. He may demand no more of his employee than that these relationships are nurtured and maybe occasionally expanded. On the other hand, a good salesman might, without upsetting any long-standing relationship, be able to motivate and excite the customer's interest to the thought that he could possibly sell a great deal more of the product than he has so far achieved. With a little creative thinking, the professional salesman should be able to advise on markets or on new ways of promoting a product. Through doing his job effectively, he would not only stimulate the business prospects for his customer, but he would be adding considerably to the earning potential of both himself and that of his employer.

It is encouraging a mere order-taker to view his activity in a different way that might turn him into a salesman and a more valuable asset to his employer - and, in the process increase his earnings through commission payments and incentive bonuses in recognition of performance.

Take the selling of books as a good example of the need for constant contact. A small publishing operation may not have on-the-ground sales representation, so it does not benefit from immediate face-to-face relationships. A curious thing happens when a bookshop goes onto computer ordering and stock control - *sales drop!*

This might seem odd, and appear to negate the reason for the technological advance. The theory of such a system is obviously that book stocks are kept topped up to a certain level all the time. As a book is sold, it is replaced. Fine, so far as that goes. However, the system only works so long as the stock level on the shelf is maintained at more than one copy! The greatest sales always occur in the shops that stock a number of copies of any particular book - and the higher that number is, the greater the resultant sales. There are two reasons for this:

1. The title is more obvious when there are more copies - the sight of several copies adds a feeling of urgency at the point of sale, suggesting the popularity of the book.
2. If only one copy is stocked, the system reorders the book when the sale is recorded. The ordering process in the book trade is very slow, and although, in some cases, an order is turned round in 24 hours by the publisher or distributor, there can still be a gap of days, if not even a week or two, when the book is not in stock or on the shelf.

Clearly, such a situation means that no sales are possible when the book is not visible on the shelf. Multiplied up, the implication is that for about half the year, in the outlets that only keep one copy of the book, that book is not available and, again multiplied up through, say, a chain of 100 shops, the resultant loss in possible sales is considerable. All this assumes, of course, that we are talking of books that enjoy a regular sale.

The point of this example is to demonstrate the importance of fostering and maintaining contact with customers to ensure that stocks are always maintained. No matter how much technology has been introduced, nothing can surpass human contact! Going back to the bookshop illustration, a telephone call will invariably produce an order - and often reveals that a book is out of stock without anyone having noticed. So, it is in the publishers own interests to constantly keep the human contact alive - simply on the basis of order-taking because, in the absence of an on-the-ground representative, this is the only way of ensuring sales levels are maintained, if not actually stimulated.

## A NEED FOR GREATER PROFESSIONALISM

My aim then - coming back to this book! - is to provide the salesman with a working system which, when completely mastered, will ensure that tangible results become the certainty, rather than the hoped-for outcome of any sales interview. If such a book had been available to me when I first went into selling, I am sure it would have made a significant difference to the speed of my development and given me a greater understanding of the *human* side of the career I was hoping to master.

My feeling is that a much greater degree of professionalism is needed. This was very much brought home to me by a remark made to me by a businessman, vulnerable to approaches by direct sales people. He was complaining about what he regarded as the dishonesty of many sales people who hide behind a variety of labels intended to suggest a professionalism many of them just do not possess. His argument was that if a person presents themselves as a *Consultant* or *an Advisor* they should have achieved a degree of professionalism to match the title. "I wouldn't mind so much if they knew what they were talking about, and, even more, if they just had some clue as to how to talk to people - if, that is, they hope to sell something." His real objection was that side-stepping the label of *salesman* is not good enough unless there is evidence of real qualifications.

The same man told me he had made a point of always asking these would-be advisors and purveyors of goods and services that were seeking his attention, how long they had been in the business. The answer rarely amounted to more than a few weeks! His feeling was that such people are doing their employers no service whatsoever, indeed they could be inflicting irreparable damage through their lack of credibility and their obvious inexperience in handling human relationships. He had asked one of his unsolicited visitors what would happen should he, as a potential customer, buy something, then in a week or two, that salesman left the company? The young man looked at him in utter surprise. "Why should that make any difference?" This hit-and-run attitude, my friend felt, did the salesman no credit at all. It simply demonstrated that there was no understanding of people and for the need people have for the security and confidence that continuity can give.

## CONTINUITY MEANS SERVICE

Customers appreciate continuity, and a great deal of good solid business is built on this concept. We all tend to grumble about the way in which high street banks are run these days. The word *manager* has taken on a new significance, indeed there are now so many of them that there seems no longer to be any continuity in relationships - the very thing the customer appreciates most of all. When putting their important affairs into the hands of the bank, the customer appreciates individual attention and it is this that provides confidence and a feeling of trust. The fact that every subsequent contact throws up yet another manager actually distresses some people. The larger institutions seem to be losing sight of simple and fundamental needs.

## QUALITY vs QUANTITY

Anyone wishing to establish and develop a sound and lasting career in sales must realise that everything has to be built on professionalism. It is vitally important to create an environment of trust and mutual respect with both prospective and active customers and to develop a relationship which implies on-going service on which the customer can rely totally.

Good salesmen are the result of good selection, recruiting and training. Recruiting for quality rather than quantity will always pay dividends in the future. Unfortunately in industries where the turnover of sales personnel is high, recruitment is usually for quantity since it is prompted by the constant need for replacement. By implication, people needing to be replaced have either failed or moved to another organisation. It is amazing to me, and an awful indictment on certain industries, that failures are constantly recycled into other companies - and all too often without much regard for the taking up or checking of references. This is simply a vicious circle where cause and effect become totally confused and the lessons never seem to be learned. If the clay is of poor quality, how can the potter hope to produce fine products of permanent value? We live in a time when the recycling of rubbish is valued as environmentally friendly - it is not, however, either friendly nor desirable to recycle poor quality salesmen to be inflicted on a trusting and unsuspecting public.

Clearly one cannot be so presumptuous as to imagine that it is possible to change everything with one magnificent stroke of the pen, but it is not too much to sincerely hope that one might have produced an idea of lasting value that could affect both ethics and creativity - and therefore prosperity.

## '*CLOSING*' IS NOT IMPORTANT!

So many books have been written on the subject of *closing the sale*. *Closing* is necessary when someone is being persuaded to do something that they don't really want to do. Selling goods and services to people who don't want them is never going to produce any lasting or on-going success. Neither is it the way to build those all-important relationships on which so much may eventually rely.

*Closing* should simply be the end result of a set of circumstances. It does not require special training or special techniques and indeed requires no particular skill. The only attribute required is an understanding of everything that comes before the so-called *close*.

I have always believed that by placing too much emphasis on the importance of *closing* endows the word with a sort of mystique which can breed uncertainty and nervousness - two ingredients that have no place in the sales process.

Those who have read any of my previous books will know that I am rather fond of using golf analogies as illustrations that work very well in explaining certain types of human behaviour. I would hasten to point out that this certainly does not imply that I am a good golfer - so let us have no false illusions about that!

In the game of golf, obviously the aim is to get a small ball into a small hole situated a long way off in the landscape. This endeavour is aided by the use of a collection of instruments designed (often it seems, inadequately!) for the purpose. Various hazards are designed into the course to make the procedure even more difficult. These hazards produce curious mental barriers as well as their more obvious physical ones. It is *how* the instruments are used that will achieve the final result in the fewest number of strokes. Getting the ball into that small hole is only the last move in a series of actions of equal importance - each one carried out as part of a whole plan, a relentless process of moving towards an eventual goal through a sequence of planned moves, which could be defined as sub-goals.

As with most things in life, success relies on adequate and accurate planning and preparation. In golf, if all the attention (the preparation) is concentrated on the ball at one's feet, it should, when struck, be delivered accurately to the desired place on the course. Anyone who has ever played golf knows that all too often this simply does not happen! But the failure is only because the preparation was not properly carried out - it has nothing to do with the clubs, the quality of the ball, the weather or the lie of the land. It is a combination of correct practical preparation coupled with the right mental attitudes that will achieve the ultimate aim.

There are blind golfers that have developed the skills necessary to be able to play the game. However, they must always be aided by a sighted player who can, as it were, set them up for a shot. Obviously the blind player is not going to be put off by the physical hazards on the course, such as a spread of water lying in the path of his shot. But his shot will be affected if the sighted player *tells him too much about the problems.* This is exactly the same in our normal or working lives. The moment hazards are pointed out, anxiety can complicate achievement.

What we are about to explore then is a system designed to prompt the salesperson into regarding each and every sale as no more than a process - a series of moves designed to advance the situation towards an eventual target in the easiest possible way. The adoption of such a game-plan will ensure that nothing is forgotten, nothing is overlooked and that the ultimate event known as a *close* is a completely natural outcome, easy, and painless.

Creativity cannot thrive in muddle or chaos. Any craftsman must learn to use the knowledge and tools of his trade in a manner that allows his thoughts to flow freely and to be translated into the creation of an end product - whether that be getting a small ball into a hole, painting a picture or making a sale. And this must be achieved without having to go through the mental process of *how do I do it?* The answer to the *why?* question helps to define intent, whilst *how?* expresses doubts about ability.

The use of acquired skills must become unconscious to allow the creative process to roam free, unfettered by limitations of the purely technical. Selling can be thoroughly creative - but only once a system has been learned and practised, so that there is a track on which to run. The techniques then become instinctive and the creative spirit is allowed to blossom.

*Selling should be fun and full of fascination
...only then will it become highly rewarding!*

# 2
# *The Rules of Engagement*

## KNOW YOUR PRODUCT
All selling must start with a product of some sort.  It may be in the form of manufactured goods or it may be a service. *And the very first requirement for any aspiring salesperson is to **know their product.***  Not just *know* it but to thoroughly *believe in it*.  The better the salesman's knowledge of, intimacy with and appreciation for the product,  the greater will be his genuine enthusiasm in selling it.  In this context, enthusiasm definitely equates to success.

It is easy to get excited about something you know intimately - impossible if your knowledge is scant and questions are feared.  Product knowledge must be so good that questions are welcomed and regarded as positive sales aids.  The salesman who regards questions as attempts to defeat him is merely demonstrating his ineptitude and insecurity.  His lack of product knowledge simply testifies to his unsuitability for the profession.

Enthusiasm is a fine spring-board but,  to develop some real skill in selling one must understand that selling is approximately 2% product knowledge and *98% **people knowledge.***  So,  despite the importance of product knowledge,  knowing your product represents only a small proportion of the learning curve you will have to go through.

## TELLING IS NOT SELLING
Selling is not a matter of trying to convince people.  They will not be convinced by any amount of arm twisting.  People

24

are convinced by honesty, integrity, enthusiasm and professionalism. Never be afraid to communicate your feelings - they will always have more value than mere words alone.

The moment a sales situation develops, certain aspects of human behaviour are triggered and stimulated into immediate action.

Selling is a subtle process, an amalgam of advances and retreats, of giving and of taking back, of knowing when to remain silent, when to push and when to back away.

One of the great myths about selling is that *a good salesman is a good talker.* How often have you heard people say *'he's a born salesman! He really does have the gift of the gab'*?

Let's get this old chestnut out of the way before we go any further! *There is no such thing as a born anything - except a baby!* And *that* is packed with potential just waiting for life to develop it!

Selling is an acquired skill - it is certainly not an inherited one. Some people might disagree with that as a definitive statement - but it could be that they think they are recognising someone as *a born salesman* when, in reality, they may merely be recognising a person with a temperament and personality that would suit the selling profession.

The proposition with which we should start is that *a good salesman must be a good listener.* Telling a prospective customer about a product is in no way selling it - unless of course he has asked for the information because he already knows he has a need for the product. If the customer doesn't recognise a need for the product, no amount of telling will

25

make him want it - and if he doesn't *want* it,  nothing will make him buy.

## NEED AND WANT

All selling revolves around one small but very significant word - *want.*

But *want* only comes about through recognition of **need** for the product.   Need can only be revealed through asking questions.   Consider this - *how can a salesman know what his customer needs unless he asks?*   And yet the mistake is made over and over again of believing that if the salesman tells his customer sufficient about the product,  he will surely want it.   **Remember,  the customer himself doesn't always know what he needs until it is demonstrated to him!**   And yet - and here is our first bit of magic - *once a need is established,  half the job is done!*

This then is where *people knowledge* comes into the picture - knowing how to approach people,  how to gain their trust and confidence and how to ask the sort of questions that will lead both the salesman and the customer towards establishing and recognising *need.*   It is logical,  straightforward and simple - providing the salesman has not taken any short cuts.

## SALES RESISTANCE

So far everything sounds fairly straight-forward,  wouldn't you agree - but wait!    There is a little thing known as *sales resistance* built into each and every one of us.   The moment we suspect that someone is trying to sell us something,  up it pops - and down come the shutters!

Sales resistance is the prospective customer's habitual state! It is donned like a suit of armour and is his natural ultimate protection. But, there has never been a defensive system that cannot be penetrated, and all suits of armour have their weak and vulnerable points - providing you know precisely where to probe.

Selling, as we have already said, is a game, but like all games, it has to be played according to certain rules, with each participant knowing and understanding his or her role. Subtlety, an understanding of people, and unobtrusive persistence, are the weapons of the salesman.

## PLAYING BY THE RULES

The game is easy to play once you realise that it is based on simple reactive responses. It is the natural thing for a human being to throw up the barricades whenever an approaching salesman is sensed.

This can be very disconcerting to the uninitiated and can produce in the inexperienced salesman, a state close to panic or fear. Fear, though, is so often the direct result of ignorance or lack of understanding, and knowledge is the weapon with which to arm oneself to overcome it. Knowing what to expect in any situation provides one with the weapons necessary for immediate combat.

The prospective customer, through long experience and a highly developed instinct, knows the rules of engagement, and at first will appear to be quite co-operative. This can very easily unseat the unsuspecting novice salesman, taking him completely off-guard and lulling him into a sense of quite false security. He must not allow himself to be influenced by this seeming acquiescence. He must bravely maintain his guard and examine his situation carefully.

Consider that situation for a moment. How did he come to be there in the first place? *He sought an appointment.* The prospective customer agreed to allow him into the house,

27

shop or office - though possibly not without the odd remark such as *'well don't think you're going to sell me anything!'* (this is really nothing more than a weak defensive ploy, almost a conditioned reflex). So, in fact, the salesman is there virtually by invitation, surely a definite plus - but the salesman must not be deceived by that because it is no indication whatsoever that the customer will buy. There are many people who will allow a salesman into their homes out of idle curiosity. There are others who will agree to the appointment because the salesman was so charming or persuasive on the telephone, but whatever the reason, it is fatal for the salesman to make any assumptions. It is merely that the first hurdle has been negotiated and the first point scored.

Remember, *the game must always be played by the rules.* The salesman should always remember that his prospective customer knows perfectly well what he is trying to do, and what the purpose of his visit is. There is absolutely no mystery, so the salesman must never permit himself to be taken in by seemingly innocent and co-operative behaviour - and he should not be put off either! *Battle has been joined and the game has commenced.*

## THE SCORING SYSTEM

Sales training often includes a lot of talk about what are known as *buying signals.* These are nothing more than *indications of agreement.* They come in a variety of forms but are all definite pointers towards the successful outcome of the sale which is, after all, what the game is all about.

The first move towards an ultimate conclusion has already taken place - being granted an appointment. Your part in the game now, having penetrated the initial defences, is to create a whole series of these pointers by following the route we recognised earlier - asking questions, seeking answers and questioning those answers always with the aim of establishing that all-important *need*. The next step is to relate that need, in your customer's mind, to the benefits of the product you are offering.

In an ideal world, transforming the customer's need into a *want* is the next step before you can arrive at the conclusion of your sale - which is, ideally, *allowing the customer to buy from you.*

The way in which points are scored in this game is through the number of times you can get your customer to say '*yes*'!

Doesn't this process suggest that there must be a plottable series of events taking place? I have called this sequence *Four-Square-Selling* because there are four vital areas or steps in the sales process, providing they are mastered, that represent the building blocks to an almost certain outcome, and that of course is the sale. Play the game by the rules and follow the patterns I am going to unfold, scoring points by watching closely for possible buying signals, and you will have embarked on a fascinating voyage of self-discovery which can be full of both fun, exhilaration, and, above all, *increased earnings!*

# 3
## *The need for a System*

**FORGET ABOUT CLOSING**

Many books have been written, audio tapes and videos produced and seminars performed on *closing sales!* - infallible methods all!

It is, however, the very existence of all this material that suggests and implies that *closing* is a problem. Why else would such a fuss be made about it?

The implication is that there is some gigantic obstacle to be overcome, some horrendous experience to be encountered and conquered. 'Systems' have been designed to come to the salesman's assistance. Complicated procedures have been evolved which, if followed assiduously and unquestioningly, 'will guarantee the closing of a sale'. The poor would-be salesman has been so bombarded with the idea that *closing is a problem*, he has become instilled with an in-built fear of closing, seeing it as some awful barrier lying across his path just waiting to defeat him at his moment of triumph. This fear of failure - for that is what this situation has produced - is sudden and certain death to any aspirations he may have nurtured to become a sales superstar. It sometimes seems to me that the plethora of material produced has created the very problem that it then seeks to solve.

It has been said that fear of failure is a great motivator - and I would not wish to argue with this as a principle. It can give an edge to the sales situation, just as stage fright can stimulate the actor's performance. But fear of failure can be a double edged sword for it can also be the reason for a salesman doing something foolish in an attempt to save a flagging situation. However, the idea that if you are not afraid to fail, you don't care sufficiently about success, has its place in the motivational arsenal.

But, in the case of *closing*, presenting an answer by creating the initial difficulty is putting the cart before the horse. If we considered the sales process as being like a staircase, carrying one upwards towards an inevitable conclusion, would you not agree that all the steps should be equal? Of course you would! And yet, the step that represents the ultimate conclusion - the dreaded *close* - is too often presented or thought of as something almost insurmountable.

*When a salesman experiences difficulty in 'closing' a sale it is almost certainly because a step was missed or left out of the logical sequence of events - the prepared and practised route that should lead towards the sale.*

## SHORT CIRCUITED

There are a number of reasons for a potential sale to be blown out. Something has been short circuited so that the customer was not in a position to enable him to make a valid decision.

He was not in possession of sufficient information because...

1. the right questions had not been asked, or
2. no *need* had been established in the customer's mind.

Alternatively, a need may *appear* to have been established but the customer may not have been given the right help to allow him to recognise that *need* before the over-anxious salesman had passed on to the next phase of the sale. In other words *the close of the sale was attempted before all the elements to ensure its success were properly assembled.* Rather like trying to close a door before it has been properly hung within its frame. And that is what *Four-Square-Selling* is designed to overcome.

## THE IMPORTANCE OF A PLANNED SEQUENCE

As a salesman, practice your art. Think about it, analyse it, become so familiar with the tools you use that nothing can disturb, disrupt or upset the creative possibilities of what you are doing.

*Four-Square-Selling* as an acquired discipline is no more than a plan, a track on which to run, providing a series of steps of equal size and importance which will eventually arrive at an inevitable conclusion. The sequence should be easy and smooth and follow a logical pattern that ensures nothing is left out and nothing is added that has no place there.

**The four squares represent:**

**1.** The appointment, arrival at the sales venue, the introduction and the establishment of empathy between the salesman and his prospective customer.

**2.** Gathering *facts and feelings* - asking the right questions to establish a *need.*

**3.** Ensuring the customer recognises need, and prompting *want* by presenting or demonstrating the product to fit the *need/want.*

**4.** Answering questions, dealing with objections and concluding the sale by allowing the customer to buy.

Selling is actually a continuous cycle. It does not simply start with a discussion and end with a purchase. The process begins literally before the salesman has even met his prospective customer, and it doesn't actually end when the goods change hands, or the contract is signed.

The starting point for the sales process is *prospecting*, sometimes followed by a certain amount of research into the background of the prospect. The more one can learn, the better equipped one is in the actual sales situation.

And, when a sale has been concluded, apparently satisfactorily, it is often necessary to *reinforce* the sale to ensure that the customer is totally happy with the outcome and contented with his purchase. This is the starting point of a continuing process, the creation of invisible momentum that will cement a relationship that could run for years. It is also part of creating what we have already called the feel-good-factor. Reinforcement of sales goes on all the time. For example, the glamorous advertisements for cars that appear in the more up-market glossy magazines and Sunday colour supplements are there as much to reinforce sales and create the feel-good-factor amongst people who have already bought the advertised car, as to catch the eye of new or prospective customers and promote more sales. For the on-going relationship with either a salesman, a company or a product, the feel-good-factor is of paramount importance.

## SCORING THE FIRST POINT

Every part of the sales process relies on the development of human relationships and on the careful build up of empathy between the parties concerned. If the salesman antagonises or upsets the prospect in any way, he is dead.

Remember the scoring system? The object is to obtain as many YESs as possible! Each YES brings the conclusion of the sale one step nearer. In securing an appointment, the salesman has already scored his first YES - his first point! It is at the appointment stage that the game begins in earnest and both parties take up their positions on either side of an invisible dividing line. Even at this early stage the prospective customer can fire a salvo or two, but the salesman must not be put off by this.

*'You can come, but don't think you are going to sell me anything!'* This means nothing at all! The prospect knows perfectly well what you do, knows that you are coming to try and sell him something, so why does he make such a remark?

### It is because he is accepting the salesman's challenge.

...it is the strike across the face with the glove! He is saying that he is prepared to take on the challenge and that if the salesman is good enough, has something to sell that is of interest, he *could* be convinced!

A prospective customer might tell the salesman who telephones him, *'you'll be wasting your time. I am a very difficult person to convince.'* The salesman *must* learn to recognise such statements as challenges. *This person is defying the salesman to try and convince him.* A timorous person might well answer a remark like that by apologising for having troubled the customer and ring off. The salesman who is on his toes will recognise the challenge and respond appropriately by saying that *he* doesn't regard it as a waste of time because he has something really worthwhile to show the customer.

**The people who make challenges of this nature, often become the very best customers!** They like to present themselves as tough nuts to crack, but that is because they are quite serious people, who, once convinced of the salesman's integrity and the worth of what he is selling, will feel confident to become his customers.

There was a life assurance salesman who rang a prospect seeking an appointment and the man said, *'I am putting the maximum away in a pension plan, I have more life assurance than I really need. All my capital is invested tax efficiently and for the best possible return and I am getting all the tax relief I can legally have. That is my answer to the average life assurance salesman!'* The salesman responded with a speed that took the customer by surprise. *'I am **not** the average life assurance salesman!'* The prospect replied with equal speed and not a little amusement, *'well then, you had better come and see me!'* The result of that encounter was some business and the beginning of a long-lasting relationship.

That is what I mean by creative thinking.

It is not an attempt to be clever, but it is turning a situation around to one's advantage in the pursuit of a particular aim. It is understanding something of human nature as well as getting past the defences in a practical, and perhaps entertaining way. Empathy was established through a seemingly simple bit of banter that had a very beneficial affect when the two men eventually met.

## PREPARE YOURSELF - VISUALISE SUCCESS!

Visualisation is a most powerful force in any human life where the attainment of goals and desires is paramount. The technique is concerned with the programming of the subconscious mind. To have a strong visual image of oneself as a successful person, to experience the *feeling* of true success, will carry you a long way towards the fulfilment of your desire. Such thinking builds up self-esteem, which in turn produces outward manifestations of an attitude which can so easily affect those around you.

Programming is very like a process of imagining and of rehearsal. On the way to an appointment, if you are able to visualise how that meeting will go, the form it will take and the outcome it will assume, your self-confidence will grow - and that, in turn, will affect the outcome of the event. Go over the sequence of events as you expect them to take place. Try also to place yourself in the shoes of the potential buyer and see the events you are visualising from his point of view. How will he perceive you? How will your product or service benefit him? Will the acquisition of your product or service bring added value to his life? Will buying from you make him feel good and attain that rosy glow that usually accompanies buying?

Visualisation must always be a very positive exercise, otherwise you could be digging your own grave. Remember the power of negative thinking is just as potent as is positive thinking. Avoid visualising anything in any way negative. The person who expects or anticipates problems, rejection or failure will ensure that those are exactly the things that will come about.

Quite recently, the results of a scientific investigation into the ways in which the brain behaves during the learning process, were published and it was suggested that, in regard to this particular function, the brain is divided into two quite distinct parts or compartments. One section is concerned with retaining learned data and producing the required information purely on recall, whilst the other section concerns itself with the learning of new skills. As a new skill is practised and rehearsed, proficiency is acquired and the learned function is passed over into the other compartment - that concerned purely with repetitive performance. The investigators had observed golfers and had arrived at the conclusion that the old adage *practice makes perfect* is truly justified. In a reasonably proficient player, the golf swing is accomplished with the minimum of delay. The information or data needed to produce a good shot is reproduced over and over again, whenever required. It comes from the brain compartment that is concerned with learned knowledge. If however, the golfer hesitates for any length of time over his drive, the thinking function is moved from the 'learned data' compartment to the 'learning' compartment - in other words the golfer reverts to being a novice at driving and, as a consequence, invariably produces a quite hopeless shot or simply misses his ball!

In visualisation, always remember the things that are likely to influence your customer most - *trust* and *professionalism,* as well as a feeling that you will provide on-going service. Your customer is, in fact, buying *you* even before the product or service you are presenting.

If you develop the habit and practice of visualisation you will be surprised how much it improves your general performance. You will feel much more in control of the interview and be able, with much greater ease, to dictate its style and pace.

## LEARN TO RELAX

Selling should be a relaxing experience! To many people it is anything but that. Think about it - anxiety and nervousness can only affect a sales situation badly. Never lose sight of the fact that *people enjoy the buying experience.* It creates the thing we have already discussed - *the feel-good-factor.*

Cast your mind back to the last time you made any major purchase. You almost certainly experienced a rosy glow of satisfaction at the decision you made.

In a sales situation, keep thoughts of this sort uppermost in your mind and realise that you are leading yourself and your prospective customer towards a rewarding experience. Should you feel nervous, these are the kind of thoughts that will allay your anxiety and allow you to relax, and through that, allow your customer to feel relaxed too. Anxiety and nervousness lead to forgetfulness and carelessness and make it very easy indeed to inadvertently side-step some vital aspect of the sales cycle. Anxiety is easily conveyed to others and can cause feelings of unrest for which they cannot easily account. Sales cannot thrive in such an atmosphere.

*Four-Square-Selling* is designed to allow all the best attitudes to develop naturally, creating an atmosphere of trust, understanding and professionalism.

## FOUR-SQUARE-SELLING

is intended to help the sales person remove all these problems by ensuring that importance is placed equally on every aspect of the sales process. This way the ultimate conclusion assumes no more importance than any other aspect of the process - it is merely the logical outcome of planned events.

The idea of the four-square concept is to help develop a mental association with the component parts that make up the sales process in a way that will ensure no element is forgotten, omitted or glossed over on the journey towards a certain conclusion. Each square, or element, as it is dealt with and mentally put into its rightful place, is as vital to the success and completion of the sale as any other. Not unlike a jig-saw puzzle, the four-square diagram (to which we will come in due course) is not complete until every piece is in its correct place. Each piece of a jig-saw means little or nothing on its own, but, once its place has been identified, it has considerable significance.

## BEWARE OF THE SIMPLICITY!

*Four-Square-Selling* is a remarkably simple concept but please don't underestimate its importance. As with all simple things, there can be a temptation to complicate it, in an attempt to make it appear more viable.

Having always been interested in cooking, I have acquired a considerable collection of books on the subject. The best are, without any doubt whatsoever, the *simplest.* Some cookery writers seem to feel a need to make everything to do with the production of good food complicated, surrounding it with a sort of mystique that in reality simply doesn't exist. The best food is produced from the finest raw materials, handled with simplicity and economy and served with the minimum of delay. It is precisely the same with selling - a good basic structure, simplicity and economy in the presentation, leading to an immediate and predictable conclusion.

Most of us, when we were children, learned a lot about spelling and word formation by assembling building bricks which had letters printed on all their faces. We learned by associating certain patterns with the sounds of words. All learning processes start in much the same way - the programming of the sub-conscious with images that trigger ideas and concepts, which, in turn, eventually become our conscious thoughts. The consolidation of the process is simply practice and rehearsal.

The *Four-Square-Selling* principle works on exactly the same basis as the building blocks we knew as children, providing the necessary visual imagery to trigger the conscious thinking process. Once the four-square diagram is embedded in the mind, a quick mental check will reveal which square is missing and therefore which part of the sales sequence has been missed, skipped, or simply overlooked.This might seem to imply that the sales process has to be a lengthy affair. Sometimes, of course, it will be, but very often everything will drop into place so quickly that the salesman is almost taken by surprise. When and if this happens, he could be in danger of killing the sale stone dead by creating an 'over-sell' because he feels that he has not done his job properly! ...but more of this later.

Selling is very much a creative process and all creative processes call for flexibility of thinking. Ask a painter how long it takes him to paint a picture and he will tell you that is an impossible question to answer. He might easily tell you that the best work he ever did, took no time at all - simply because everything dropped into place effortlessly. The time a painting takes bears no relationship to its worth or its aesthetic value. It could be said that every creative act relies for its success on everything that has gone before. It is the sum total of the artist's experience up to that moment. Sometimes all the elements come together swiftly and easily. At other times hours of laborious toil produce results only fit for the wastebin.

As the painter must master his tools to the point that their use is instinctive, so the salesman must be totally familiar with his product and have a sales plan at his finger tips with which he is so familiar that it is second nature to him. *Four-Square-Selling,* as a systematic prompter, will ensure that this happens.

So now it would seem appropriate that we take an in-depth look at *Four-Square-Selling...*

# SECTION 2

## *The Four-Square-Sales System*

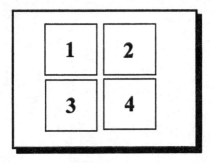

# 4
## *The Sales Cycle*

**GETTING THE APPOINTMENT**

This is all part of the game, and a preliminary exercise to the sales cycle itself  The salesman's aim must be to strike that delicate balance between intriguing his potential customer into wanting, or, at the very least agreeing to see him, yet without telling him so much that he, the customer, is able to make a judgmental decision that would, to him at least, make the salesman's visit pointless.  As a famous American salesman once said, *'if I tell, I'm dead!'*  In contacting a prospect, be it a business or an individual, always remember, *all you are selling is an appointment.*  Never, never try to sell your product over the telephone - that is discounting, of course, the concept of telephone sales - when no follow-up visit is planned - as this involves another sort of approach altogether.

In seeking an appointment, the really soft sell is very effective.  This I have always thought of as the give-and-take-back technique.

*'Maybe I can be of help to you - maybe I can't!  We will only know by meeting.'*

*'My product has been of great benefit to lots of people - but maybe it won't suit you.  If you don't like what you see, nothing is lost.'*

*'Even if you like what I have to show you, you don't have to do anything about it - the decision is entirely yours.'*

It is approaches like this that minimise feelings of any sort of pressure and make the prospect feel relaxed and confident that he is not going to be pushed into a sale.  It is very important to avoid asking questions that invite a negative answer.    Remember the scoring system!    Points are scored for YES answers.   To give you an example, never ask:

*'May I come and show you the latest XXX lawn mower?'*

The almost certain and predictable response would be a fairly emphatic *'No!    I already have a mower...'* etc.   Such a question - inviting a negative reply as a natural response - throws up an immediate barrier,  and once that barrier has been erected,  it is very difficult to get past.    In fact,  it is virtually impossible.

A better response would be:

*'Do you have a lot of grass to cut?'*

The answer poses no problems and can only elicit a straight forward YES or NO - or,  better still,  a flood of remarks giving you a clue to the prospect's feelings towards grass cutting!   Either way,  you have produced interest and opened up a conversational channel.   The answer might also be of use to you as a mowing machine salesman, since it could give a clue to  which of your products could be the most appropriate to show your customer.

It would then be logical to continue with other questions, asking whether your prospect *enjoys* grass cutting,  what sort of machine he is currently using and how long he has had it. Is he satisfied with his present machine?   When did he last consider making a change? (Not,  you notice, has he ever considered making a change? - which would elicit a NO answer)   There are a dozen natural questions that could be asked by way of developing and broadening out the conversation, but make a rule of not  prolonging the contact any longer than it actually takes to secure the appointment, otherwise you could be running the danger of telling too much and getting the negative answer you are seeking to avoid.

Things can always be brought to their conclusion by adding something like...*'well perhaps I could drop round sometime and show you the XXX?     There's nothing like seeing the thing working - and if you don't like what you see, you don't have to do a thing about it!   The decision is entirely yours...'*

What could be more reasonable than that?     There is no pressure.     There is no implied obligation.     There is no secrecy - and the customer has been told it is entirely his decision.     He has nothing to lose.     It would be almost churlish of him to say NO!

Sometimes the natural and instinctive defence mechanism will cause your prospect to make some seemingly aggressive or outrageous remark.   This is nothing more than a last-ditch stand and is very easy to counter - just show surprise!   *'That's very interesting - why do you say that?'*

In an odd sort of way,  that is quite flattering!   You have told the man he is interesting.   Everyone enjoys that.   Often, in explaining his remark he will,   without realising it, completely defuse his own aggression and become quite reasonable,  even friendly.

Politicians often employ this technique when an interviewer has asked an awkward or embarrassing question. *'Now that is a very interesting question,'*  the politician says with real warmth and sincerity.   The interviewer immediately feels good whilst the politician goes on to neatly side-step the issue!   I am not in any way suggesting this is what *you* should do...

Another defensively aggressive counter may go something like this - *'You are the fourth person this week who has tried to sell me...'*

Now this is either a gross exaggeration or simply quite untrue.   What you must always bear in mind is that you may have timed your telephone call very badly without even being aware of the fact. A key piece of machinery has just broken down at a critical moment when a job had to be finished and your prospect is not in a very receptive frame of mind. But however his aggression came about, it deserves a good response delivered in a friendly, light-hearted manner. Remember, there is almost certainly nothing personal in his attitude so do not allow it to get to you. *'Well the other three obviously didn't get to see you! Am I going to be the fortunate one? After all, if you don't like what I show you, you don't have to do anything about it. The decision is entirely yours.'* Very often this sort of approach not only takes the heat out of the situation, but it can even amuse the customer into giving you the appointment, despite his current frustrations.

As I am sure you are aware, there is danger in dealing with some situations in the ways I have suggested, and not everyone could do it successfully. It requires a good understanding of people and an awareness of the fragility of the situation. To go too far or over-step the mark could be fatal to the sales situation - or ruin a potential relationship for all time. It requires the ability to read the temperature of the water at all times and the skill to remain in charge, no matter how the conversation develops.

Allow me to repeat once more, *your sole aim is to secure an appointment.* You are not selling a product. The golden rule is to keep all such calls as short and to the point as possible - and don't *tell* too much or you could be pushing your prospect into saying NO, he doesn't want to see you.

## REJECTION
Every salesman, indeed, every person, no matter what their occupation or status, dislikes rejection in any form. It is the

salesman's greatest fear, and as such, something which is very undermining. We are all vulnerable to rejection simply because it is our natural state to want to be liked.

Many people don't really appreciate what this fear is until they experience it for the first time - and some never get over the experience.

Rejection should be looked on as merely an expected part of the salesman's life. NOs will always appear, so one must be ready to accept a number before the significant YES arrives. Rejection has its own scale, relative to how much each NO means to us. Sometimes NOs are quite insignificant, even to be expected, and so the effect they have on us in minimal. They still, nevertheless, represent a form of rejection, if only of an idea. The nature of rejection is such that, in the business context, it is rarely a personal thing, and should not be taken as such - it is an idea, a product, a service that is being rejected, not necessarily the individual offering that product or service.

Human beings, however, are very frail and vulnerable when sensitive issues arise, and the tendency is usually to take rejection in a very personal way. To understand a situation is often to be able easily to control it or at least to come to terms with it. If rejection was such a big deal, none of us would every get married or form lasting and meaningful relationships. And yet there are people who are so affected by rejection that they carry the results of it about with them like so much excess baggage.

Think of it this way - unless you are totally obnoxious, there is absolutely nothing personal about rejection in a sales situation. It is not *you* as an individual that is the target of the perceived rejection. It could be you as a *salesman* though - never forget the salesman does have an image that is not especially acceptable to many people.

So much comes down to the manner in which the initial confrontation is conducted - that very first impression. First impressions are *so* important - there is great truth in the saying that *you only get one chance to make a first impression!* It has always surprised me that there are so many companies willing to employ totally inadequate telephonists on their incoming switchboard. The person who answers the telephone is the *very first contact* the caller has with that company and his perception of that company could be strongly influenced by the initial image he receives. The telephonist's role is very important when thought of in this way because a great deal - perhaps literally! - could hang on that first impression.

If you ever suspect that rejection might be the result of your own behaviour, I suggest you take a long hard look at yourself because you might be dropping into habits that can only multiply and get worse. Habits can always be modified or changed if noticed in good time, when it might only require a bit of fine tuning to put things right. If habits get too embedded it is far more difficult to 'unlearn' behavioural patterns and replace them with new or modified ones.

## GETTING THINGS IN PERSPECTIVE

In a sales career it is important to get rejection into its correct perspective. Think of what you do, what you are paid for. Your real purpose is *to get people to make decisions*. It doesn't really matter whether the decision is a YES or a NO. You are getting paid whichever way it goes.

There are bound to be so many NOs to every YES.

There was a racing system going the rounds some years ago that was based, not as one might expect, on form or on the inside knowledge of racing tipsters, but actually on the tipsters themselves and the statistical likelihood of them being right or wrong. From daily records each was given a rating - say, for example, 5. This indicated that the particular tipster would be wrong 5 times before he was right. So, after following the tipster of your choice, waiting for him to clock up 5 incorrect forecasts, you then placed your bet, in the statistical 'certainty' that his next tip would be correct. So many NOs before a YES!

To overcome the possibility of rejection, the salesman can protect himself with statistics so that NOs simply become the stepping stones on the journey towards YESs.

Suppose each sale you make is worth £50.00 in commission and your records show that you have to call on 5 people on average to make that one sale. Then, on that statistical basis, every call you make is worth £10.00 whether the answer is a YES or a NO. In other words *you are being paid for rejection!* Looked at in that way, rejection is just part of the job, part of the thrill of the chase.

## THE REAL SALES CYCLE

Following the very simple diagram on the title page to this section, the cycle of the sales process is as follows:

1. Taking up positions - introduction to the encounter, immediate initial assessments and the setting-up of an appointment.
2. The appointment. Settling in, getting acquainted and establishing empathy. Assessing *style* of buyer.
3. Fact and feeling session based on *identified style* of buyer - seeking where his *Feel-Good-Factor* might lie.
4. Matching likely benefits to established needs.

Making a decision as to the best course of action - or the most appropriate product to offer to promote the maximum *FGF* - followed by the product presentation.

*Conclude the game in a way that promotes*
*the maximum rosy glow for both parties...*

## Square 1.  THE INITIAL ENCOUNTER

Have you ever considered what happens when two strangers meet face-to-face for the very first time in a sales situation? There are four basic elements that come into play absolutely instantaneously...

    **A.** How *you* see the person you are confronting.
    **B.** How *they* see *you.*
    **C.** How *you* see *yourself.*
    **D.** How *they* see *themselves.*

This surely is *communication* at its most confusing!   All the senses are on tip-toe,   assessing and evaluating,   making assumptions (often quite wildly) based on immediate visual impressions,  body language and speech patterns,  as the two parties confront each other across the deep,  natural gulf that initially separates them.   Diagramatically,  what is happening is something like this...

| A | B |
|---|---|
| Cautious<br>Defensive<br>Obstructive<br>Stubborn<br>Condescending | Intimidating<br>Dangerous<br>Suspicious<br>Sharp<br>Unreliable |
| Smart<br>Professional<br>Reliable<br>Concerned<br>Ethical | Wise<br>Knowledgeable<br>Logical<br>Intelligent<br>Open-minded |
| C | D |

You can add your own words to those I have chosen to put into the four sections of the diagram,  but the end result will be about the same - *chaos!*  The initial impressions, over-laid of course by pre-conceived notions which might have been formed from a previous telephone encounter,  are so opposing as to appear,   when considered in this way,  almost insurmountable.    And yet,  from that very first moment, through words and gestures,  immediate adjustments
start to be made and the fine-tuning necessary to form any acceptable relationship goes on until some sort of common ground is reached.

This might be described as either a state of empathy or merely as an uneasy and temporary truce awaiting further evidence to amplify acceptance or rejection.

This exercise demonstrates the complexity of what might,  at first sight,  seem to be a fairly simple situation.   More than that, it goes to show the importance of working at the relationship and attempting to refine it before launching into any formal business discussions. The easier and more relaxed the relationship, the easier will be the natural outcome - and don't forget how the points are scored! *The YESs will only come when some degree of empathy has been established.*

## BEWARE THE SALESMAN

There is, as we have already observed, a public perception of the *salesman* essentially as someone of whom to be wary. A little 'sharp' perhaps, a master of the flamboyant, given to over-flowery description, possibly even a shade untrustworthy? - using that word in its truest sense - *not worthy of one's trust.*

Clearly it is imperative to establish *trust* at the very outset. The salesman must be forgiven for expecting that his acceptance would be both immediate and automatic, but after looking at the diagram of initial confrontation, you would doubtless agree that nothing can ever be assumed!

## HOW *DO* OTHERS SEE YOU?

How others see you is very much linked to your own self-image, though the two pictures do not always match in quite the way you might hope. Social and cultural differences can often cloud the issue as - and I am afraid we cannot side-step this - we are all affected by both class and economic differences and the values one person accepts may at times be greatly at variance with those of the person they are confronting. It is very true that *we appear as we are.*

There are certain types of people that the majority of us would judge on appearance to be basically untrustworthy, whilst there are others that appear to evoke feelings of respect, admiration, sympathy, empathy or trust.

It is almost impossible for human beings, on initial confrontation, to avoid signalling information about themselves - and information about how they are reacting to the person before them. We all provide a visual display of our attitudes by both word, action and unconscious gesture. It is virtually impossible to avoid displaying or tying on the labels of type, character and maybe also occupation, that are so easily read by others. It is a mix of these visible as well as the intangible signals by which you will be judged, assessed and eventually pigeonholed by others. That is not to say they have got everything right! We all tend to make quick and spontaneous assessments of others, often to realise later that time does not always confirm these initial judgements.

Whilst some of us will shun the idea of making signals to others that provide instant labels, others, probably through a sense of insecurity, want to provide as much information as possible about themselves and display it to the world at large.

We do not all interpret signals in the same way. The things we wish to say about ourselves can sometimes have a double edge. What has great meaning to one person, may mean nothing, or perhaps mean something quite different to another - the result of some social or cultural difference.

An industry has grown up to exploit personal image through public exposure, making it easy for the self-publicist to enjoy telling the world a whole range of things about himself. Remember the craze for his and her names over the windscreen of a car? Car stickers and T-shirts now tell the world where one has been, what one has seen and what one's sexual preferences are - particularly with reference to occupation.

Television has shown us the car we should drive if we wish to be perceived as a particular type of person. We know what clothes we should wear, we know what to eat and drink, what sports to play and where to take our holidays. In fact everything is catalogued to make it easy for the non-original individual to become part of the non-original mass.

If someone said of you, *'would you buy a second-hand car from that person?'* - how would you react? Would you be annoyed? Would you resent the question and see it as a personal criticism?- because, as we would all recognise, that stock question is simply indicating that the person making the remark thinks you look untrustworthy. But *why?* What is it that prompts the remark and why should you feel offended?

When it comes to self-image, it would seem we are marching through a mine field! Could it be that we have no idea of the image we present to the world - no matter how we over-lay it with recognisable symbols for others to read? How can we be sure that the symbols *we* accept as expressing the message we want to give will be read as we intend them?

*Are we capable of assessing how others may see us?*

## SELF- IMAGE

Anyone who has attended a large motivational rally - events very common in the selling world - will have seen presentations made by gentlemen hung about with gold bracelets, expensive watches and all the other icons popularly associated with success. The speaker is broadcasting one message, but whilst *some* of his audience might read it in the way it is intended, others may be receiving another, quite different message. Once again, we may be looking at social and cultural differences.

Presenting an image that can, within limits, be 'read' does have its advantages - but only so long as it doesn't lead you into trying to perform to some standard that is not natural to you, and with which you may not be comfortable. Just as the genuine article is recognisable, the imitator makes himself much more visible than he ever imagines.

Never attempt to play up or down to people in the mistaken idea that you are making *them* feel comfortable, for be sure you will come unstuck! You will always be most comfortable as your natural self - any attempt to play roles that you may imagine will suit the person you are talking to is inevitably courting disaster. Once a person is perceived as either false or bogus, all credibility is lost for ever.

*'This above all, to thine own self be true, and it will follow as the night the day, thou canst not then be false to any man.'* - *William Shakespeare*

## BELIEVE IN YOURSELF

Personal attitude plays a great part in the creation of image. If you are to be successful at anything in life you must have a high degree of belief in your own ability to succeed. Your potential is only affected by the limitations that you place on yourself.

*The values you place on yourself*
*will be the values others will accept.*

There is no doubt about it, people are attracted to what they recognise as success. So, if you *feel* successful, the likelihood is that you will *appear* successful. Presenting yourself as a well-packaged, successful person can promote great confidence in the people you meet.

We live in an age where the badges of class have largely disappeared and people can no longer be categorised quite so easily by dress, accent and manner. This can result in some very confusing messages!

People will usually accept you at the face value you place on yourself, the image you project will dictate the way in which you are treated.

There are salesmen who always park their car out of sight when making a call, surely an indication that they are aware of the effect the vehicle might have on their personal image. There are others, of course, who will park their car in the most obvious place, for exactly the same reason. There are those, too, who might have done better to park their personality around the corner! Unfortunately we have been brain-washed by advertising into the belief that cars express status.

### *It is personality that expresses status, integrity and professionalism*

It is a pity that we should have to place such importance on these matters, since life ought to be concerned with more worthwhile issues. However, our social system has ensured that daily life has become encrusted with biases and pointers that immediately tell others what is *right* or *wrong* about us. And, of course, those two words, in themselves, are interpreted in so many different ways as to render them very nearly meaningless. It is for this reason only that I think it worth making one or two observations that might head off problems right at the outset of a sales encounter.

It has been demonstrated by behavioural psychologists that the majority of people will place more trust in a person dressed in dark rather than light clothing. The dark suit with black shoes commands the most respect. It is immediately recognised as the archetype of the professional image.

The cars we drive are great indicators of implied status, attitude and success - or the lack of it. However, we are dealing here with an expensive item , and it might not always be possible to drive the car we would ideally choose to drive. Whatever the car, it can at least always be clean!

On the matter of dress and personal presentation, flexibility of attitude is more important than following rigid rules. There are times when, in the sales context, it might be totally inappropriate to present oneself in a dark suit - for example if one was selling agricultural machinery to farmers. Gumboots and a waterproof jacket would more easily fit the occasion - and be regarded more seriously by the farmer/customer.

Dress, it is said, is the attire of the body, whilst words are the attire of the mind.

*The badly dressed person will be remembered for his clothes
- the well dressed person will be remembered for himself.*

## MOTIVATION vs MANIPULATION

*A warning!* I would like to emphasise one thing very strongly indeed - *the aspects of selling that we are about to explore have absolutely nothing to do with the manipulation of people in any way.*

Manipulation is a nasty word, especially within the context of selling, and I would suggest that you put it right out of your mind. I have likened selling to a game, and the playing of a game suggests there must be a *winner* and a loser. I am not for one moment suggesting that, on making a sale, the salesman is a *winner* as that would suggest, by implication, that the buyer is a *loser.*

*That would go against the whole philosophy
of Four-Square-Selling.*

Both buyer and seller are winners - *the playing of the 'game' is merely a symbolic ritual - a battle of wits, if you prefer it, to achieve an end that will be to the benefit of each.* The word *manipulation* implies the taking of unfair advantage through some form of trickery or acquired skill. The salesman's job is not, in any way, to manipulate.

### *It is to motivate the customer into making a decision*

It is to motivate in the sense that the salesman's aim should be to provide the encouragement and stimulation the customer needs to consider a product or a proposition, recognise that he has a need for it, and then to take the appropriate action by making a decision.

## Square 2.  FACTS AND FEELINGS

Imagine, for a moment, that you are on your way to an important sales appointment with a new prospective customer. You are asked to make a choice between two boxes of information about that person which could be of help to you - one is labelled *FACTS* and the other labelled *FEELINGS*. Which box would you choose?

*Facts* are merely the answers to straight forward questions, and it is easy for anyone to collect information of that sort just by asking. *Feelings,* however, are rather different. They are often the result of questioning the answers to *fact-finding* questions. They represent an overlay of extra, more privileged, and often quite invaluable information, as a bonus to the fact-finding question - emotions and opinions that might not have been revealed at all unless the *feeling* question was posed.

*Feelings* are the *why,* the *how,* the *when* and the *if.*

In making your choice then, if you were to arrive at your meeting armed with the box of *feelings,* you would be in a position to immediately understand your customer - and, more importantly, to understand the motivational forces that prompt his thinking. Only when you are in possession of both *facts and feelings* can you truly assess your customer's likely needs and wants. A great deal of your job would be done and your brownie points would be piling up fast!

Fact-finding then is asking straight forward questions, seeking purely practical information and establishing the basics of your customer's situation.

*'What do you do for a living?'*

The answer is a *fact.*

*'Do you enjoy it?'* - *'Is there anything in life you would rather have done?'*

These are *feeling* questions, capable of providing access to a flood of information which will give an insight into aspects of personality, attitude, aspirations, hopes and dreams - vital clues to an individual's deeper feelings and the true pointers to *need.*

## EFFECTIVE COMMUNICATION

What is selling but communicating?    Selling requires communication of the highest order.    As we have seen, selling is about establishing relationships and creating empathy before the passing of information regarding a product or service is a viable proposition.

This passing of information must be achieved in as clear and concise a manner as possible since it is by the quality of the information that your customer will be enabled to evaluate the product before making the vital decision - to buy, or not to buy.

In the conveying of messages (information) there is ample scope for misunderstanding of the most basic sort.

Consider this...

*I speak...*

*I know what I mean to say...*

*...but am I saying what I mean?*

*You hear my words...*

*but do you hear what I think I am saying?*

*-or, do you hear what you want or expect to hear?*

One of the greatest barriers to understanding can be the human mind itself, and its habit of constantly jumping to conclusions through its ability to make instant comparisons by endlessly referring to past experience in the busy process of checking and evaluating.

Communication is the bridge between people's minds so, for it to function at its best, it relies on all our senses - speech, sound, sight and feelings, and of course, even touch.

How do you like to be treated by other people?  Do you think other people get the most out of you when they treat you *the way you want to be treated* - or the way you feel you *should* be treated?   They will know how best to treat you by the way in which you are treating them. Attitudes in communication are often very reciprocal. Treat people with kindness and consideration, and that is the style of treatment you will get in return.

### *If you want to gather honey, don't kick over the beehive!*

Asking questions and seeking answers is obviously dependant upon good communication, and that can involve several of our senses.

Communication is a matter of both speaking, listening and watching, as our attitudes and physical behaviour in the conversational context can add a great deal to the simple spoken word. The study of *body language* is fascinating, and to be recommended to anyone interested in human behaviour.

The subject deserves a book on its own, and of course there are good books on the subject which are well worth investigating.

Words are the result of thought processes, but body language is the result of sub-conscious emotion and empathy. Just like the difference between the answers to fact and feeling questions, there may be a simple factual answer to a posed question, seemingly requiring no more than a few words. But watch! - for *body language* may unconsciously add the *feeling* answer at the same time as the spoken word is providing the *factual* answer.

The interpretation of body language is *the art of seeing what others are thinking.* We all indulge in unconscious tell-tale physical gestures - indeed, we cannot help making them - and the trained eye can easily read and interpret their true meaning.

Scientific research has demonstrated that the total impact of a message is about 7% verbal (i.e. through the words employed), 38% vocal (tone of voice, inflection etc.) and 55% non-verbal. When we have that uneasy feeling that someone has told us a lie, it is almost certainly because we are aware unconsciously that their words and gestures did not tally in conveying the same message.

We all use body language to emphasise certain points in conversation. Take the wagging and pointing finger of the speech-maker, or the clenched fist that thumps the rostrum. In a sales situation, when the customer's attention might seem to have wavered, if one leans forward towards him, a sudden sense of urgency is imparted and his attention will immediately return, often to be seen as a mirroring of your gesture as he in turn leans forward towards you.

In the interview situation, posture will always show who is in charge - who is interviewing who.

Try to avoid sitting back in a very comfortable chair. The relaxed position will not only visually spell out a lack of urgency, but the sheer comfort your body is experiencing will have the effect of making your presentation too casual, too lacking in urgency. You may also be conveying the message to your customer that you intend to stay for some time! Rather, sit on the edge of your chair in a position that suggests alertness and not having time to waste.

You could of course stage-manage your own behaviour by first settling into the chair comfortably whilst you casually establish a degree of empathy with your customer. To then sit up, changing your position, acts as a signal, demanding attention and giving importance and emphasis to the presentation you are about to make.

## WOMEN AND BODY LANGUAGE
Women are particularly good at using body language. In the sexual and social context they are able to create exactly the

mood and message they wish to convey. They have a head start over the mere male but need to be very aware of this in a business context to ensure that confusing messages and signals are not transmitted which could work against them in the creation of a sale.

Women are often regarded as better negotiators than men. That mystical thing we call *feminine intuition* is really a heightened ability to interpret non-verbal communication - vital in negotiating - and this ability is said to be even more acutely established in women who have had children. For some women motherhood has made them so practised in non-verbal communication during the early years of bringing up their infants that this skill is still valuable in later life.

Selling is only a form of negotiating and I have always believed that women can be very good indeed in the profession - but more of this later.

## THE VALUE OF SILENCE

When it is important that you know as much as possible about your prospective customer, silence can be your greatest ally.

Having asked a question and listened carefully and attentively to the answer, continue to be attentive, but remain silent, looking at your prospect with interest and anticipation. Most people instinctively dislike silences in circumstances like this, and their natural inclination is to want to break it. Providing it is not you who breaks it, your prospect certainly will - and will tell you much more by way of answer to your original question.

Questioning the answers to questions will also stimulate people into greater frankness - as we have seen, this is the route to *feeling* questions, following a series of facts. That trusted stand-by of a question, *'that's interesting - why do you say that?'* will invariably supply further information.

## EMPATHY AND INTEREST

Establishing a good rapport as soon as possible with your customer is most important - everyone likes to be the centre of attraction. To show real interest in your customer and what he or she does is the surest way of gaining their confidence and establishing the right sort of empathy. In the past I often invested time in being shown an entire manufacturing process by the owner of a business simply because I had asked a question - how something worked, or what someone was doing. Business men love to be asked how their business came into being. I recall once visiting a small factory on an industrial estate and meeting the owner on the shop floor. There was a machine nearby and I just happened to ask what it was actually making. The owner went into a long and interesting explanation before he gave me a complete tour of the factory which lasted three quarters of an hour. At the end of this time we had become really well acquainted - and yet he didn't actually know my name or what I had called about! When I was able to explain the purpose of my visit, such empathy was already established, my job was easy.

## THE HABIT OF LISTENING

Fact-finding must never appear to be an inquisition. It should be easy, relaxed and conversational. The whole aim of fact-finding is to paint a back-drop against which the context of the sale is played out. You need as clear a picture as possible before you are in any way equipped to advise your customer over anything. Remember, you are working your way towards establishing a *need*, and it is unlikely you will achieve that without a good deal of information, amplified, of course, by your customer's *feelings*.

Acquire the *habit of listening*. Everyone knows that old adage *you have two ears and one mouth, use them in that proportion!* But how many of us are really good at following that sound advice? Can you, hand on heart, claim you are a really good listener?

It has been said that listening is an acquired skill. Many people will confess that they feel they don't really know how to talk to others easily. They will admit that they could do with some training in communication skills - by which they usually mean, speaking to people.

### *But have you ever heard anyone say they don't know how to listen?*

We human beings are very strange creatures! It is an odd quirk of human nature to remember a good listener as a good conversationalist! We all enjoy talking about ourselves. The salesman's job is to encourage people to talk, whilst he assumes the more passive role of interested listener. At the beginning of this book I mentioned the popular image of the salesman as *having the gift of the gab.* Perhaps - and this is a sincere hope - I have now convinced you that the good salesman is really, in fact, a good listener.

But a word of warning - the roles must never be allowed to reverse. If your customer talks about his summer holiday at great length, *listen,* no matter how boring it may be. On no account start telling him about *your* summer holiday!

The customer must always be allowed the star role. Never forget, the outcome of the intended encounter is that he is going to be allowed to buy from you. You must grant him every indulgence, whilst you remain firmly in the supporting role - but always in charge of the situation, simply keeping it on track.

## BEWARE - THERE ARE DANGERS!

As a salesman's skills develop it is very easy, unless he is aware of the dangers, for him to take advantage of his customer, possibly quite inadvertently. Selling becomes very easy to some people and they develop a sort of sixth sense for the use of emotive power both through speech and body language. Some trainers and motivators are very fond of the use of what they call, *power phrases*. Unless we are very careful indeed, with thoughts like that, we are getting a little close to *manipulation*. If the salesman's belief in his product is total, and he follows the guide lines of *Four-Square-Selling*, there will never be a need to employ any form of manipulative behaviour.

Manipulation is the resort of the bad salesman. Once any form of bad, unnecessary or unethical behaviour starts to become a habit it will lead to other problems - short cuts and malpractices - resulting in a complete loss of credibility, loss of that all-important feeling of self-esteem, and, as damaging as anything else, loss of earning power.

## Square 3. NEED - WANT

Need is a strange little word with so many meanings and so much innuendo. Generally, in the context of the sales situation, *need* implies that the product or service on offer would be of use, value or benefit to the prospective customer - but it is possible that it may not always be apparent to either party that an obvious need actually exists. It is for this reason that it is important to go through a thorough and professional fact-finding exercise.

## WARNING!

*Never assume that because you can see what you think is a need, that there actually is one. Unless your customer can see it as well, it is no more than a fiction of your own imagining.*

Good fact-finding will always uncover need if it genuinely exists. Need cannot easily be created - remember *telling is not selling - and need must be recognised by the customer.*

*Need* has other, perhaps less obvious connotations. Any psychologist may tell you that human beings are totally bound up with and by fundamental needs, and an understanding of these could be useful to the creative salesman, so let's have a look at the most obvious.

# THE VALUE OF HUMAN NEEDS

## *Needs related to self development*
These are often regarded as the most important of all human needs and include anything that loosely falls into the realms of *improvement for good* - improving knowledge or expanding outlook and widening horizons. I have mentioned *the-feel-good-factor* - and that would certainly fall into this category.

## *The need for esteem*
Self-image is of tremendous importance to each one of us. We all have a basic need to be seen by others, and indeed, by ourselves, in a favourable light. We have a deep fundamental desire for recognition - particularly the recognition that endows us with status, in the sight of our peers. But status has its own language and imagery. It can be suggested, often somewhat dubiously, by symbols - visible signals that are recognisable by others as the indicators of affluence, position or standing. The car, the house, the way you dress - your visible life-style.

## *Social needs*
These are the needs related to love and a sense of belonging. Security that comes through personal relationships, the bonding that is the outcome of love and affection. The sense of being a part of something, such as membership of a club - these are all the things that produce a strong sense of security of tenure. *The need for being needed.*

## *The need for safety and security*
Security and protection. We all have a need to feel safe from both physical harm, personal injury and illness, as well as a

need for the security of home, employment and possessions. We need to feel that our position in the world is secure and that we have erected both physical and psychological defences around ourselves as a protection against possible violation or harm.

### *Physiological needs*
The need to fulfil and maintain all our physical and practical requirements and avoid the possibility of hunger, thirst, or warmth.

Even this very basic understanding of human needs has significance to our sales situation. Within the context of any sale, several of these fundamental needs may be appropriate to our customer at any one time. Your customer may, for example, feel that ownership of your product might somehow provide him with added status. Or it could be that some safety angle of your product interests or impresses him. Or perhaps he recognises that his general physical well-being will be enhanced by the product or service you are offering.

Once, through fact-finding, these things have become apparent, they are very strong pluses in establishing general need. Matching the benefits of the product to the attitudes of the customer is a powerful way to demonstrate and establish need.

It is not necessary for you to feel that you have to do all the work - allow the customer to establish a series of needs for himself. Ask him what he would demand of a product such as yours, and develop your theme from his answers.

## WANT IS JUST AROUND THE CORNER
Once the need for a product or service is firmly established in your customer's mind, it is a simple matter to move to the

next phase of the cycle and begin to present some of the benefits your product can offer to best match your prospects perceived requirements.   Now that his need has been recognised and confirmed,  and it is clear that your product can go a long way towards satisfying it,  *want* is only a few paces away.

## Square 4.  WANT TO SALE
Beware!   There is a possible snag at every turn!
Never assume that because someone has admitted that they have a *need* of your product that they automatically want it!

Admittedly *want* is very often only a step away from *need* - but remember the game that is in progress.   In admitting need the customer's natural and unconscious defensive instincts might be aroused again and he may be prepared to fight a last rearguard action!   Remember *objections*?   This is one of the points in the sales cycle where it is almost traditional to toss a few objections,  like hand grenades,  into the peace and tranquillity of the situation you thought you had produced.
Perhaps now you are beginning to see how important it is *never to take anything for granted* in the sales situation - and, of even more importance,  never to cut corners or try to

short-circuit any part of the sequence of events that a sale *must* pass through. This, of course, is the very essence of *Four-Square-Selling* - the very heart of the matter.

## DEALING WITH THE HAND GRENADES

You really can defuse these in your own mind immediately, because - providing you are confident in your product knowledge - objections are actually *nothing more than buying signals*! And, as such, they are very easy to overcome.

Never mistake a request for information for an objection or you could find you have a *real* objection on your hands. Questions, demands for information, and even what might seem like a criticism of your product, are all probably buying signals. All that is being said is *'give me the answer to this and I will buy the product.'*

Many salesmen feel sick in their stomachs at the idea of having to deal with objections. This is another area where some trainers have made too much of the situation and produced an in-built worry for the novice salesman, even before he has encountered the event. Fear of having to deal with objections comes only second to fear of rejection.

But, there is absolutely nothing to fear if you are prepared for the possibility of objections and if you are totally confident in your product knowledge. If you know your product intimately, believe in it and, even more importantly, believe in yourself, you will be in total control, literally welcoming objections and seeing them as stepping stones to completing the sale. Remember what we said before - *objections are plus situations,* opportunities to score bonus points in the game in which you are involved. They simply allow you to bend with the wind and amplify details that perhaps you did not make sufficiently clear earlier in the cycle.

Once the hand grenades have been defused, you will have a greater insight into your customer's requirements. A second plus is that, in your customer's eyes, your status will have been enhanced, whilst, in your own case, your self-esteem and self-confidence will have increased.

## SHOW SYMPATHY AND UNDERSTANDING

Make the customer feel pleased about having raised a good point - give him *status* and raise *his* level of self-esteem too. *'That's a very good point, Mr.Smith - I'm glad you brought it up.'* Have you ever noticed how politicians use ploys of this sort when asked a question by an interviewer that is a bit too close for comfort? Sometimes you can hear the interviewer almost preening himself after this suggestion of his cleverness in asking such an astute and intelligent question. And whilst he is still basking in his enjoyment, the politician nimbly side-steps the issue and avoids answering anything too awkward.

Always try to see things from your customer's point of view - he will love you for it. Try to put yourself in his shoes and, by doing so, carry him further into his own objection so that he can see you understand his concern.

*Never* argue or disagree with your customer. Do not, above all, push against his objections or ever dismiss them lightly. They are points of importance to him and anything that even remotely seems like a frivolous attitude will go against you. The only way to get the best from a disagreement is to avoid it completely. The only way to win a person over to your way of thinking is to respect his point of view and demonstrate your understanding of his concern.

Allow him to do most of the talking and he will very likely form the conclusion that buying your product *was his idea.*

## PRESENTATION/DEMONSTRATION
After answering objections and questions, it is easy and natural to slide into a simple demonstration of your product.

*Want* may already have been made obvious through questions about price and delivery. But, if the product has not already been demonstrated, doing that will almost certainly clinch the *want* - if not the actual deal itself.

Selling is especially easy if you have real and genuine enthusiasm about your product. Enthusiasm is infectious and transmits itself to others - but never let enthusiasm get the better of you. Remember *always* that *telling is not selling.* Boring the pants off your customer by getting too enthusiastic and going into too much detail *too soon* can easily cause terminal loss of interest!

The only point at which the customer will be totally interested in detail is when *he has decided he wants the product.* At that point you could hardly tell him too much, because *now* he genuinely wants to know everything.

## PRODUCT vs SERVICE
Selling a service is very different to selling a tangible product, but so far as the human aspects of a sales situation go, there is very little difference. The product salesman has the advantage of selling a visible object that can be touched and handled, demonstrated and experienced. He is able to explain that the product comes in different sizes and a variety of finishes and colours, so the customer is more easily able to make a decision.

The service salesman has the problem of dealing with an abstract concept which can neither be seen nor touched. The selling of life assurance is a good example - and that is even further complicated by the fact that *nobody actually wants it*! The selling of life assurance is one of the most difficult of sales tasks, and, as such, represents a particularly good example of many of the most common sales problems.

Everyone *needs* the product, but nobody *wants* it. Most people will admit to themselves that they know full well that they should have their lives protected for the benefit of their dependants, but there is a reluctance to do anything about it. For this reason, perhaps, it has always been recognised in the financial services industry that *nobody **buys** life assurance, it must be **sold** to them.* Could it be that we all suffer from delusions of immortality? The life assurance salesman has to act as the still small voice of conscience to bring the need out into the open and thereby create an environment of genuine recognition and want.

If it is true that people want what the product can do for them, you have the clue to the way the sale must go - it is *feeling* questions that will lead towards demonstrating need and want. Lecturing the client on all the options and technicalities of the policy would kill the possibility of a sale in no time at all.

In the financial services industry, the proposal form represents an ideal vehicle for not only obtaining the required information, but also for *providing* information. For example, there will be various sections on such a form that ask specific questions relative to options offered by the policy. These give the salesman the opportunity to tell the client a lot about the policy - information that would have been difficult, even tedious, to impart during the sales cycle, for fear of saying too much. All he need do when such an option is reached, is lay down his pen and point out to the client that they have reached a point where he has a decision to make. Since the client has clearly, by this time, decided that he wants the policy, any extra information is going to be of real interest, because it concerns *his* policy - and that is something about which he now wants as much detail as possible.

Take great care never to fall into the trap of over-familiarity. I am not talking here about taking liberties with your customer, but rather, becoming so familiar with your product or service as to assume that your customer sees it as clearly as you do. Always start from basics and build with logic, then assumptions can never lead you astray. Spend *as much time as it takes* to be certain your customer has a full appreciation of the product. The simple rules are...

- Don't give lectures
- Encourage questions.
- Allow the customer to find some things out for himself.
- Listen!

Only when you are *certain* that your customer is completely satisfied with your answers should you make any move to bring the matter to a conclusion. If you have done everything correctly, your customer, by this time, should be ready and happy to buy from you - need has been recognised and want has arrived!

Briefly sum up the points that have been covered, then ask '*is there anything else I should have told you - or anything else you would like to ask?*' Answer the question - if there is one - and the job is done! '*Are you quite happy then?*'

If you try to push the conclusion before the customer is ready, be sure that *it will not work*! If you can spot the signs in time, go back to asking if there is anything else the customer wants to know and reinforce whatever you may have missed or skimped.

Don't forget that everyone is not the same. In Section 3 there is a system for identifying types or styles of character which should, once you are truly familiar with it, enable you to treat people in the way that their particular style demands. Beware too of *over-selling* for it can produce uneasiness, irritation and suspicion. It tends to build a kind of anxiety.

As Shakespeare said -
*'...methinks he doth protest too much!'*

but as some other wise person once remarked -
*'...the more he protests his honesty,*
*the faster I count the teaspoons!'*

# 5

## *The point at which the sale concludes...*

...and it is surprising just how many sales have been squandered at this stage!

I do hope that by leading you through the process we have examined, you would agree there is absolutely no reason why anyone should feel even the slightest degree of fear or apprehension at bringing the game to its natural conclusion by securing the sale.

And yet, as I pointed out right at the beginning of this book, *there is a fear.* Remember all those books, tapes and seminars devoted to *closing sales* - each one offering its own infallible method? I would say again that placing so much emphasis on this thing called *closing* implies a problem which, approached in the right way, as I hope I have now amply demonstrated, just *does not exist.*

I make no apology for returning to that golfing analogy yet again, for it presents such a good example to make the point that cannot be stressed to strongly - the very heart of the *Four-Square-Selling* concept. When the golf ball is struck it either lands in the intended area, or comes to rest at some totally unexpected and unintended spot. This fact can obviously present the golfer with either a plus, or a resounding minus - and a problem!

The ball that flies straight and true only does so because of all the physical and mental preparation that went into the shot. The player was concentrating totally on *what he was doing there and then,* and *not* on where the ball was intended to go.   Naturally, at the start,   that decision had to be made, but,  after that,  all the emphasis was on the preparation and concentration needed to make the necessary shot.

### *It is exactly the same in selling!*

In his anxiety,   the salesman often places far too much emphasis on the final outcome - *closing the sale* - rather than concentrating all his attention on *NOW* - what is happening *at this moment* to ensure that all the correct things are being done to ensure nothing is missed or overlooked.

### *It is the same in every aspect of our lives.*

We spend time endlessly *hoping and wishing* for things to happen rather than *visualising* what we want to achieve, building up the *desire* to achieve it,   then applying the *massive action* that will be needed to ensure the goal is reached.    Once there is desire for achievement,  it is only action that will bring the result.   I became fascinated by this concept whilst writing *'Believe you can!'* ,  a book devoted to the idea that anyone can achieve *anything* or *become anything they truly want to become.*

A lot of the blame for the attitudes of some salesmen can be laid at the doorstep of employers who - often quite unnecessarily - pressurise their sales force by means of competition.

Sales managers set targets which are intended to *stretch* the salesmen and encourage them to attain new peaks of performance.   This is perfectly acceptable,  *providing the manager understands the people under his control.*   Some will flourish and thrive under the pressure of competition whereas others will experience dejection and anxiety. You may argue that these are the people who should not be in selling at all - and of course you may be right. However, let us not forget that 3% figure I quoted earlier. There are many people in sales who are not really suited to the profession which, in some areas of business, is so hungry for new recruits, as to be willing to take on almost anyone. My hope is that if even the mediocre salesman can be persuaded by the *Four-Square-Selling* system to look at the job in a different way, they will not only find their own real measure of success, they will feel happier and more relaxed in what they are doing - *and that is then bound to be reflected in the earnings they achieve.*

## LOGIC AND REASON

If you have read this far and you still believe there is a problem in closing - no, sorry! *in bringing the sale to its conclusion* - you have missed the whole point of *Four-Square-Selling.*

If the process has been followed properly, the right preparation has been made, and the mental exercise of ensuring that each square is in place in its correct position, *the job is finished,* a sale has been created and a customer has been allowed to buy from you!

Now where is the difficulty in that? There simply isn't one!

If the sale will *not* come to a satisfactory conclusion, it can only be for one of the following reasons...

- No *need* was established.
- No *want* was created.
- No money!

The entire sales process is nothing more than *logic and reason*, with every step the same size. And yet the timorous salesman, full of in-built apprehension about *closing* and about bringing, like an obedient dog, a sale back to his manager, creates insurmountable obstacles out of his imagination and places them across his own path. Such insecurity!

If you don't like the idea of abandoning the salesman's favourite word, *closing*, I had better present *my* claim for the infallible method of doing just that. This is tried and tested and comes to you absolutely free of charge. Providing you know everything has been done properly, all you have to do is *ASK!*

*'Anything else I can tell you?'*
*'Shall we make out the order?'*
*'Shall we do the paperwork and set things in motion?'*
*'Do you think that will do the job for you?'*
*'Which colour would you like?'*
*'Would you like me to order one for you?'*
*'How soon would you like to have it delivered?'*
*'Are you quite happy about that?'*
*'To complete this form, may I ask you a few more questions?'*

The questions you could ask are endless. The whole point is, *they **must** be asked* - and in exactly the same conversational tone you have used throughout the entire interview. Nothing should be, or need be different in any way - and everything must be relaxed and easy. The game is now almost concluded and you are about to score the final point!

Sales have been lost because the salesman couldn't or wouldn't bring things to their conclusion by just asking for the order.

## THE 'LOST' SALE

Salesmen love talking about *losing* a sale.    This is utter nonsense!

### *You cannot lose what you never had!*

They are deluding themselves by using the word *lost* - and deluding anyone else foolish enough to listen to them.    The implication is that the deal was struck,    everything was satisfactorily completed and then,    suddenly,    the great bombshell - the sale flew out of the window!

If you should ever feel tempted to tell these 'got-away' stories,  do yourself a favour - *don't!*   Be honest about it - *the sale was never made* because either the product wasn't good enough,  or,  far more likely...

### *the salesman wasn't good enough.*

## BEWARE THE *OVER-SELL*

It is so important to recognise when a sale has completed - to be able to read the signals that indicate quite clearly that your customer is ready to buy,  sign the contract,  or place an order. The thrill of the moment has caused many a bright young hopeful - who *did* spot all the signs - to go prattling on, carried away by his own excitement,    enthusing and eulogising over his product to the point where he has so bored his customer,  all possibility of the sale has evaporated and been lost for ever.   *That* really is a lost sale.

The sales process is only like firmly closing a door. Most doorways have,    as part of their construction,    a doorstop - something against which the door presses when it is in the closed position.   But there is such a thing as a swing door - a door with nothing to stop it being pushed right through the frame into the open position again.

**81**

There was obviously a point at which the natural sale could have taken place, yet over-anxiety, usually manifesting itself through the salesman talking too much and not being sufficiently sensitive to recognise when the sale has reached its natural conclusion, has blown out the whole thing. All that was required was for the salesman to *shut up!*

Remember - *two ears, one mouth?* To the average person, knowing when to stop talking can be quite difficult. In our anxiety to put across our point and impress our message on others, we often tend to over-state the message.

We cannot stop talking, and go on *over-selling* until we have pushed the door wide open again instead of firmly closing it. Put another way, we have bored our audience into disinterest, and have failed to make the conversational sale which was our intention.

Over-selling in daily relationships happens all the time. We are all prone to it in the belief that we haven't put our message across with sufficient clarity. Politicians are great examples of people who regularly indulge in the over-sell. The danger is that their audience can so easily become bored to the extent that they switch off - and at that point, the speaker has blown all possibility of making his sale.

The bad salesman, again through over-anxiety, pushes his luck in harassing his customer with too much contact until he antagonises his subject into rejecting him outright. Over-selling causes stress to both the salesman and his customer. Over-selling in everyday life has much the same effect - not always necessarily causing distress, but certainly resulting in annoyance and possibly indifference.

Being alert to the possibility of over-selling, both in the sales situation and in your everyday life, is the surest way of avoiding the hazard. You can *see*, through the other person's body language when you are over-selling - that far-away glazed look comes into their eyes and their gaze, along with their attention, often wanders! Read the signs...

There is a story about a man who went to see his psychiatrist in a state of considerable anxiety and stress - because of a recurring dream that worried him. In this dream, he would mount a long flight of stairs towards a closed door. He always grasped the handle and pushed with all his might, but the door would never budge. The psychiatrist told his patient to go home, and the next time he had the dream, to look very objectively at the door and its surrounds and note everything in detail.

The following day, the patient came rushing into the psychiatrist's consulting room in a state of great excitement.

*'I have been through the door!'* he exclaimed.

*'And how did you manage that?'* the psychiatrist asked.

*'I looked, just as you said, and there was a little sign that said **pull**!'*

## THE FRUSTRATED BUYER

Yet another danger! A potential customer can quite easily become frustrated because he is not being given sufficient help towards making his decision - the conclusion he actually wants - when it should be abundantly clear to the salesman that everything is in place to bring the sale to a conclusion.

Never forget that *selling is a motivational experience,* and the salesman's role is that of motivator. The customer does not need *persuading* or *manipulating,* **he simply needs motivating into doing the thing he knows he is going to do.**

But sometimes, the salesman just will not help him - and this is often born out of the fear that, if he pushes too hard, the sale will be lost. He resorts to feeble remarks such as, *'Perhaps you would like time to think it over for a few days?'*

This, of course, knowing what we have learned about the strange ways of the subconscious, is allowing the customer's natural submerged instincts to behave in a totally predictable manner. The alert sounds, deep in the customer's subconscious, like a distant bugle call to retreat, and he seizes the proffered last straw. Here is his chance to be let off the hook! This reaction, in reality, is certainly not what the customer intended, but, human nature being what it is, both parties heave a great sigh of relief and decide to leave the matter there for a few days. The salesman hastily departs, revelling in the idea that he certainly *didn't lose that one!* He didn't have to ask the dangerous question, but will have a second chance in a few days' time when the customer has made up his mind.

But the whole point is, the customer really had made up his mind and just needed the right motivation to make his purchase. After the salesman has dashed away, the customer begins to wonder just what the visit was about, and cannot understand why he feels so frustrated.

Over the following few days, the salesman builds up his hopes again, until, by the time he contacts his prospective customer, all the accumulated anxiety within him comes flooding down the telephone - only to alert the customer's survival instincts yet again. Almost before he has time to realise what he is saying, he tells the salesman he has thought things over and decided not to go ahead - *sorry!*

And that last little word makes our foolish salesman actually feel good. Well, it was all done so nicely, and he has built a really good relationship for the future.

***Rubbish!*** Everything has been wasted. Time, planning, research, effort - *everything* - and it need never have happened.

## BUYING SIGNALS

I have already made several mentions of *buying signals*, but there could be some people reading this who are still unclear as to exactly what these are, and how to recognise them.

Think for a moment. What is the most obvious buying signal of all? The answer is simple - *genuine, obvious and enthusiastic interest.* We would all, I sincerely hope, recognise that and respond to it accordingly in bringing things to a swift and immediate conclusion by allowing our customer to buy! It would be pointless, and appear to the customer as rather foolish, if the salesman persisted in going through his newly learned *Four-Square-Selling* routine. Flexibility is the name of the game. Always be ready for a short-circuit that can bring a conclusion much sooner than expected. Questions about delivery dates, colour, size, the finish of a product are such obvious buying signals, that it would be a very inattentive person who missed them!

Once *the rules of engagement* are understood, you will realise that the defence mechanism can still function right up to the very last moment! One of the classic buying signals can appear when the customer, sometimes quite aggressively, throws a positive barrage of hand grenades into the middle of the proceedings. As we have seen, all he is really indicating is that, if you satisfy him on every one of these points, you have completed your sale.

Remember, never feel threatened by questions of this sort - they are very positive buying signals. Now you may ask why these signals have to be given. Why cannot the customer come out in the open and simply declare his intention to buy? The answer is that we are dealing with *human beings,* and they just do not always conform to the actions that might seem most obvious.

Sometimes, of course, the customer *will* be very positive - but one of the things many human beings often have difficulty with is *commitment*. It is for this reason that we play verbal games which allow us to temporarily side-step immediate issues and yet still allow for the possibility of being lead (motivated) towards some inevitable conclusion - *but without loss of face.*

This is a concept we have always tended to attribute to Middle and Far Eastern peoples in particular, and yet it is something which holds great relevance to all human beings. Loss of dignity is fundamentally unacceptable to most of us. Being seen to *lose*, or to allow the other person win does not make us feel good! Psychological games are our natural defence - a way of acceding to a situation in an acceptable fashion with all our dignity intact.

So, play the game by the rules, use *Four-Square-Selling* to allow your customer *to buy from you...*

# 6
# *After the sale...*

*'Your reputation begins **after** the sale.'*

We have taken a long look at the attitudes that beset the inexperienced salesman and have discussed many of his fears and insecurities.

For such a person, there is a temptation, once a sale has been made, to pack up quickly and rush away, dancing metaphorically down the garden path, out of sheer relief, aglow with the rush of adrenaline his triumph has caused. But, his anxiety to depart could also be the result of an unconscious fear that the customer might change his mind.

Of course, this is always possible, though fairly unlikely. This is why it is always a good idea to sit back and relax after a sale is complete and spend a little time consolidating what has happened - *but without being boring about it!* This will always be time well-spent in the long term. It allows the customer to get to know you better. It provides an opportunity for setting up possible further business for the future.

But there is another, more important reason for this consolidation. Since both selling *and* buying are emotional experiences, quite an electric atmosphere may well have been created, so a little time spent in unwinding would do no harm. It is very easy for a customer, if abandoned too quickly after buying, to begin to have second thoughts and wonder whether they were too hasty in their decision. The answer then is this gentle unwinding process that really cements both the sale and the relationship.

## MULTIPLE SALES

It could be that during an interview, through fact and feeling questions, more than one need may have surfaced and been cmentally noted by the salesman. He should, in his own mind, now decide which of these needs to follow as being the most important in order of immediate priority.

This presents us with a very important rule -
*never try to sell more than one concept at a time*
- for you will certainly end up with no sale at all!

Coming back to the post-sale euphoria, it would be very easy to say to your customer something like *'I'm pleased we were able to deal with that for you. Sometime we should look at...'* and you would mention the second most important thing on your list of priorities. It is quite conceivable that the customer, in his rosy glow of self-satisfaction, could easily respond by suggesting you tell him about the next item there and then - *and there could be your second sale!* I remember a salesman who, as an all-time best, built a chain of four sales, one after the other, by following this simple principle.

*The most likely time to make a sale*
*is when you have just made one!*

## THE THEORY OF MULTIPLE SALES

The principle of multiple sales is based very much on taking *needs* one at a time and dealing with each before moving on to the next. This is very different from trying to make more than one sale at the same time - that simply does not work! When presented with too much choice, most people find it difficult to make a decision. If an attempt is made to make more than one sale at the same time, the likelihood is that no sale will be made at all!

The simple rule is...
*the more uncomplicated the choice,*
*the more certain the decision*

Deal with one sale at a time and *complete everything* - order forms,   payments,   the signing of documents - before even hinting at the second need.

Perhaps now you appreciate the importance of not dashing away as soon as a sale has been completed.   Even when there is no possibility of extra business,  don't be in too much of a hurry to leave.    If your customer offers you any sort of refreshment,  accept it.   You may have another appointment on the other side of town,  but don't worry.   Ask to use the telephone  and explain the delay to your next customer.

*The sale you have gained is more important*
*than the one you hope to make...*

...and you could damage the goodwill and empathy that has been created by seeming to be in a hurry to leave.

Your customer,  after the buying experience,  is feeling good about himself and what he has just done.   Don't,  as I have said,  do anything that might leave him wondering if he did the right thing.   A little reinforcement is all he needs,  and a few minutes for the charged atmosphere to release some of the build up of energy.   Abandoning your new customer too quickly could leave him stranded on an emotional high from which he can only descend downwards,  possibly through a veil of doubt and misgiving about what he has done.   Help him, then,  to come down to earth before you depart.   This way you will have left everything in a secure state and cemented a valuable relationship.

It is just as important to end your visit on a positive note as it was to begin it that way. A sale doesn't end when the money changes hands. The sale is the start of a much longer, on-going relationship of service and, hopefully, further business. The hit-and-run salesman is constantly having to find new customers as he will rarely return to the scene of his doubtful triumphs. Every time you acquire a new customer you are adding to a your client base for the future, which will eventually make life much easier.

## *IF* YOU DON'T MAKE A SALE...

Your reputation depends so much on the image you have created, on your attitude, and on your professionalism that if occasionally you don't make a sale, you should come away with something equally valuable - *referred leads* to other people, or other businesses.

### *Referred leads are the very life-blood of prospecting.*

Once the habit of asking has been learned, referred leads can have the affect of cutting your work in half and doubling your rewards. Please believe it! It is said that the least you should ever come away with from any appointment, is two referred leads - names of people willingly given, with permission from the donor to use his name by way of introduction. When referred leads are given to you it is a real mark of confidence on the part of the donor. It is a good rule never to use such leads *without* mentioning where you obtained the name. Apart from any other reason, the use of your initial contact can give the introduction great credibility. As a simple courtesy, keep your informant in the picture by letting him know you contacted the person he suggested - not the outcome of course, as that could be seen as betraying a confidence. These little actions will go a long way to establishing your reputation as someone both reliable and ethical.

In your view, what would be the main reason that anyone should favour your product or service over the product or service of your competitors? I would very much hope that your unqualified answer would be - *you,* because of the relationship you have carefully developed between yourself and your customer. You should have left a feeling behind you that will be the starting point for your next visit. You should leave a feeling with your customer, if you have done your job well, that you are the first person he will naturally turn to when he has problems that fall within your orbit.

## WHAT IS GOOD SERVICE?
Good service is, first and foremost, about being a real professional, and...

***being a professional is doing what you say you will do.***

Good record keeping is the key to good service. You have devoted a great deal of energy, effort and even expense to building up your customer base. It is your greatest asset towards the development of future business, therefore it is of the greatest importance that customers are contacted on a regular and planned basis. Take care to establish the right balance between never letting your customer feel neglected and not contacting him so often that you become a nuisance.

***Good service is the result of good record-keeping.***

Your customer must *never* run out of your product - if you are in the business of selling consumer goods. There are always people like you representing your competitors who could be knocking on his door. Or, if he finds himself low in stock, he could easily revert to a supplier he used before you came along and charmed him off his perch!

### *Never rely on customers telephoning to re-order.*

It is *you* who is offering the service and it is *you* who is expected to maintain it. So, a good record-keeping system is invaluable in ensuring that nobody and nothing ever gets forgotten. Even when you are selling a once-in-a-blue-moon product, such as a car, with no immediate likelihood of repeat business, there is always the possibility that you may be able to introduce something new at some time in the future. And, never forget that any customer can always be a source of those all-important referred leads - the introduction to other people like himself. You can, incidentally, always judge the quality of referred leads by the fact that people will invariably refer you to people very much like themselves in terms of income and life-style.

So, keep in touch, keep deepening and widening your relationships with customers, for you never know what the future may hold.

Years ago, when I first moved out of London, I used the services of a country estate agent and, through him, very soon found the right property. It seemed to me that he went out of his way to smooth the path and make the whole experience of house purchase as easy as possible. Three weeks after we moved into our new home, we received a letter from the agent hoping we had settled in comfortably and that we were pleased with out purchase. Almost certainly this letter was only prompted by a well-devised system and was, to him, very much a standard letter. The fact is, it was a great piece of public relations work in reinforcing the sale and promoting the agency as a caring organisation. Other letters followed, always perfectly timed, and again, their purpose was obvious - but they worked. Years later, using the same agent again, he was following exactly the same practices. This may not strike you as particularly remarkable, but the point I want to make is that, with all the good intentions in the world, such systems often become eroded by time. Corners get cut, possibly for cost saving, without realising the value of these entrenched habits.

*If something works - keep doing it!*
*You cannot re-invent the wheel.*


## SUMMING UP...

During the years I was involved in selling I lectured many new recruits on what I considered to be one of the most fundamental and important aspects of the career on which they were about to embark - the distinction that I have already made between *motivation and manipulation.*

As I hope this book has demonstrated, most selling techniques are based on a sound knowledge of the ways in which people behave in certain definable situations. I have presented selling as a *game* and talked of *the rules of engagement.* This was in no way intended to be facetious. It is a convenient way in which to present the psychology of the sales situation - an environment that must be comprehended so that the salesman recognises the need to motivate his *potential* customer into becoming an *actual* customer as easily and painlessly as possible.

None of us is able to resist behaving in certain predictable ways within the defined limits of certain situations. If we accept this, and allow that *sales resistance*, as a part of the human defensive mechanism, is inevitable, it is perfectly reasonable for counter-moves to be developed as a means of defeating this behaviour.

Everyone should always be prepared to accept responsibility for themselves and their actions, and in the sales situation, the prospective customer has every right, in his own defence, not only to discourage further moves in the game, but to bring proceedings to a halt at any time with a firm NO!

So, in summary, *manipulation* is to attempt to influence a person into doing something against their will, whilst *motivation* is to help a person to come to a decision over which they possibly need a little assistance.

# SECTION 3

## _The Salesman's Tool Box_

# 7

## *Understanding the way they tick*

**FOUR BASIC STYLES**

Several systems have been devised to categorise people into types or styles, but, happily, human beings refuse to be too neatly pigeon-holed. It is encouraging to realise that there are plenty of people who defy having the labels of convenience tied to them - and yet it is interesting to observe that, generally speaking - for that is all we can hope to do - there *are* four basic styles of personality, and it is remarkable to find just how closely the majority of people approximate to these divisions.

Obviously in selling, anything that can add to a clearer understanding of the basic persona of the individual before you is going to be of considerable advantage in assessing how best to approach them. Within the four basic types or styles, each category calls for treatment of a quite specific nature. Knowledge of this is useful, not just as an aide to achieving an immediate sale satisfactory to both parties, but for the building of the right sort of empathic relationship, important to producing on-going general sales success.

Here then is a short guide to the four main *styles* of personality, as well as some pointers towards the ways in which each category might be treated to get the best response from them.

The headings I have given the four basic types are these...

- *Dynamic*
- *Emotional*
- *Friendly*
- *Analytical*

Now quite obviously it is not possible for us to instantly identify into which quartile in this scheme of things any specific person falls. If you can familiarise yourself with the basic characteristics below, you will soon develop a skill for pin-pointing certain definite features which do tend to provide fairly clear pointers. It is frequently said of *body language* that one gesture cannot by itself identify a message - it is *clusters* of gestures that may be read as significant, when observed together. A parallel situation governs the recognition of style. One pointer will not categorise anyone but one has to have a starting point. Once the first clue has been identified, it can be checked and verified against other observable attributes or characteristics that will aid the process of identification. In other words, just as with body language, we need to look for *clusters* of identifying features to give us the whole picture.

Let's now take each category in turn and list their identifying features. You will notice, in particular, that each style operates *within a very specific time-scale* (#4 in each list) and this is of particular relevance to the sales situation.

### *Dynamic*
1. Quick reactions. Alert. Sharp, accurate decisions.
2. Not very concerned about the feelings of others.
3. Keen not to show any lack of self-control/loss of face.
4. Everything must happen *NOW*.
5. Always ready/willing to implement immediate action.
6. Does not easily tolerate laziness or inaction.

## Emotional
1. Quick reactions.
2. Dislikes routine.
3. Strives to involve others whenever possible.
4. Everything will happen in the *FUTURE*.
5. Tends towards impulsive action.
6. Shies away from isolation.  Needs involvement.

## Friendly
1. Reaction are careful and unhurried.
2. Desire always to relate to others.  Wants to be liked.
3. Favours effective change.
4. Lives very much in the *PRESENT*.
5. Enjoys the support and involvement of others.
6. Will avoid conflict of any sort.

## Analytical
1. Slow to react.
2. Puts a lot of energy into organisation.
3. Not very concerned with relationships.
4. Everything has a *HISTORICAL* time frame.
5. Plans every action with caution.
6. Does not seek or want involvement.

Because we all tend to fall into these seemingly predictable patterns, once identified,  there are clearly certain ways in which we should and should not treat one another if we wish to attain the maximum benefit from a relationship.

For example,  it would be foolish,  having identified someone as *Analytical,* to then press for an immediate decision.  This person, tied,  as they are to their *historical* time frame,  is going to require time to consider the pros and cons before any kind of answer will be forthcoming.  They will want a lot of detailed information and will not, under any circumstances, be hurried. Treating them in the wrong way will have only one effect - withdrawl and obstinate disinterest.

On the other hand, once you have identified a *Dynamic* person, you can be sure that an immediate decision will be made, and woebetide the salesman who cannot deliver the goods there and then!

Let's now look at the ways in which we can best deal with people in each of the four categories.

## *Dynamic*

These people have no time for woolliness and certainly no time for any form of frivolity or time-wasting. You are there on business, and that is all you are going to be allowed to discuss. Be accurate, be informative but not long-winded - and, above all, stick to the point. Preparation and organisation should be the corner stones of your presentation.

The type of questions these people appreciate are straight forward *WHAT?* questions.

Do not argue or you will have lost the battle! In the same way, do not try to side with them. They are not interested in forming any sort of relationship with you. It is facts for or against that they want. Objectives and results are their motivation, so stick to facts.

## *Emotional*

You can safely regard your visit as something of a social occasion and relate to these people in a more personal way. If they offer you refreshment, take it. Don't be afraid to indulge in a bit of social chit-chat, for they will enjoy it.

Aim to ensure that your approach supports their dreams. Empathise with their intuitions. They love talking about people, so stick to *WHO?* questions. Seek to uncover their opinions and relate any examples you wish to make to people - especially people they may know or know of - and the more well-known, the better! Keep things on the move and try to let your visit be fun. Don't get too detailed - they would probably appreciate details in writing far more than long explanations being provided there and then. They love special offers and incentives and are often willing to take risks, if the offer appears to be sufficiently interesting!


### *Friendly*

Be friendly and agreeable too with these people. They enjoy the casual and the informal, and like others to take an interest in them - even to accepting the occasional personal comment. Find common ground. It is particularly important to *listen* to these people and show your response to what they have to say. On no account be aggressive, threatening or noisy, but find as many areas of agreement - or disagreement - as quickly as possible, and share them. It is important to identify with people of this disposition, and to share opinions on a personal basis. Ask *HOW?* questions. They want minimum risk and maximum guarantees with a sense of on-going service.


### *Analytical*

Prepare well, be accurate, be sure of your facts and stick strictly to business. Show awareness of their need to consider things in depth. They will want all the pros and cons as well as evidence to back-up everything you may say. Ask *WHY?* questions. Be prepared to take time to follow things through in logical progression. Where agreement is reached, follow through to a natural conclusion - but if a disagreement occurs,  present your side of the case with as much logic and reason as you can muster.

## THE UNIQUENESS OF THE INDIVIDUAL

As I mentioned in my introduction,  *selling is said to be roughly 98% knowledge of and understanding of people!*

Having presented you with a way of identifying the style of an individual,  I must stress again that people just will not be pigeon-holed!    All systems that claim to be able to categorise people rely very much on the intelligence of the person using the system.   As with astrology,  based as it is on the movement of planets and their relative positions at any given time,    the accuracy of prediction is determined by interpretation.

It is only possible to tie labels on people *in the most general way.*    Never forget that every single one of us is totally unique.    There has never been anyone just like you before,   and there never will be anyone just like you again. We all have points of reference to many systems,  but there are always definable differences which are,  happily,  the aspects of our uniqueness.    Systems are only capable of presenting guide lines,   so use them as no more than indicators - and marvel at the subtleties of the human race!

# 8

# *The Four Box Record System*

I have already mentioned the importance of record keeping.

If one is to provide good, professional and on-going service, and therefore maintain the continuity of sales, it is essential to have a system that can ensure nothing is forgotten.

Clearly, in these days of highly sophisticated computerised systems, the answer lies at your finger tips. But not everyone has access to, or the skills to operate, a computer system, so a good manual procedure is needed.

Such a system is *The Four Box System* - and I now pass it on to you..

The system is based on a series of card file boxes such as one might buy anywhere - ideally in a neutral colour but with one red box - cards and section dividers for each box. The boxes are as follows...

      1. The general client file.
      2. The calendar box.
      3. The month box.
      4. The Hot Box.
      ...let's take a look at each in turn...

## 1. THE GENERAL CLIENT FILE

This is exactly what the name implies. As time goes by, this file will grow and overflow into several boxes. It is a file, not just of customer cards, but of cards for future prospects too - people or businesses that have been contacted, and, although no immediate business resulted, their records are retained for the future development and expansion of your customer base.

The cards are filed alphabetically,    the file having divisions for each letter of the alphabet.   Each individual or business has its own card - or,  if there has been a lot of activity,   series of cards - showing name, address,  phone and fax numbers,   names of buyers/managers etc. - whatever is important to the needs of the particular salesman.   The file is no more than a storage place for records that are not currently or immanently active.

The cards used throughout the whole system   are colour coded,  the colours denoting whether sales have taken place, or simply where contact was made,  interest was shown,  but no immediate action is appropriate.   They are by no means dead records,  and should be reviewed from time to time.

The most appropriate colours for coding would be red and green.   If you were to employ those little coloured, self-adhesive rectangular labels,  attaching  them over the top edge of the cards,  they can easily be identified on looking into the card file box or visible which ever way up the cards may be if they are out of the file.   Red denotes a customer who has bought,  green,  a prospect that might buy at some time in the future.

All the basic information is kept on the front of the card, whilst the reverse side is used for a record of visits and/or contacts,   and the results.     It is always worth keeping *feeling-type information.*   Reserve a space on the card for little personal details about your customer or prospect.   Small nuggets of information that will always identify that person or business in your own mind,  but that might also be invaluable when next you meet the customer.   Odd little things such as *the dog had a bandaged foot,*  or your customer's *office was in the middle of being painted,  or that he was going on holiday the following day* - any little thing to which you can refer at some future date. This gives a sense of continuity and a feeling that you take an interest in your customers. So, just before an appointment, refresh your memory from the file card, especially on the *feeling* details.

## 2. THE CALENDAR BOX

This is a box with 12 divisions, one for each month of the year. The card for any customer with whom you may have a long-standing appointment, or appointments on a regular basis, would be lodged in the slot relating to the month in which you should see him next.

There will be times when a potential customer asks you to contact him, say next November, for some particular reason. His card would be extracted from the *General Client File (1)* and placed in the November slot within the *Calendar File (2)*. It doesn't matter what date in November your meeting will be, it simply goes in the November section, that slot being for the whole month.

If, when you contact him in May, your customer suggests you ring him again in July, wherever his card might be in the system, out it comes to be up-dated and put in the July slot. Again, if you were reviewing your *General Client File* on the basis of the green tags denoting possible future interest, you may decide to extract some cards to go into the *Calendar File*, say for next month.

So, as the year progresses the slots for the months yet to come slowly fill up with potential business. As the last few months of the year come round and contacting dates for the following year begin to be recorded, the cards simply go into the vacated month slots at the front of the box so that the continuous cycle is maintained.

## 3. THE MONTH BOX

This is the real *working box.* It is divided into slots numbered 1 to 31, in other words, a slot for each day of the current month. On the first day of a new month, all the cards that have accumulated in *The Calendar Box (2)* for that month are transferred to *The Month Box* and sorted into appropriate date slots to the action that has to be taken. There will almost certainly already be some cards in *The Month Box* that were put there during the previous month when appointments had been made, a sale had taken place, and a call-back in a week or so is necessary. There are many reasons for *The Month Box* being the most active box in the system.

One of the salesman's greatest fears is of having nothing to do and nobody to contact. Really they are very insecure people, and prone to suffer from a variety of ailments such as *call reluctance, big case itis,* and most commonly of all, *end-of-the-world-syndrome.* This last manifests itself in a belief that somebody has thrown a switch or pulled a plug and the world has suddenly and irrevocably been emptied of people! Admittedly this is the hall mark of the disorganised salesman who has failed to keep all the balls in the air by constant prospecting.

*The Month Box,* then, is the greatest comfort to any salesman! It will ensure a level of activity that totally precludes the possibility of suffering any of those nasty ailments mentioned above. It will keep him motivated and on his toes, and, above all, maintain a very consistent level of earnings.

In the competitive environment of a sales office, as each month ends everyone, no matter how well or badly they may have performed, goes back to square one. It is then that *The Month Box* is a veritable treasure chest, a cornucopia of good things just waiting to be exploited. It gives the month a flying start with all the motivation that is needed - and just at the time that, because a month had wound down to its end, energy levels were low. Believe me, *The Month Box* has a great deal going for it!

## 4. THE HOT BOX

As the name suggests, this is also a box with potential!

Prospecting - of which more in the next chapter - is a continuous process during which the salesman is constantly uncovering interesting situations full of possibility. These are all worth recording, so a file card with all the details is placed in *The Hot Box* - alphabetically or geographically, whichever is appropriate to the salesman's particular requirements.

*The Hot Box* is the salesman's gold mine! Whenever he needs to push up his level of activity, it can yield up a whole new seam of rich potential just waiting to be developed. There is no doubt about it, *The Hot Box* should definitely be *red!*

So, as you can see, the *Four Box Record System* acts as a life-line to this fascinating, insecure yet motivated person, the professional salesman. It keeps him on track, for without a track to run on, he has nowhere to go...

# 9
## *Prospecting for gold*

In the most simplistic terms *prospecting* is nothing more than *finding people to see*. That sounds easy enough, doesn't it? Well, in a sense, it is, but not without a degree of planning, some hard work, and a great deal of commitment.

In the great old days of pioneering, many brave souls ventured forth, often into the wildest places on earth, with their sights firmly fixed on the single burning idea of becoming seriously rich. They were gold prospectors, men with a dream, a pick and shovel, and little else, except for an inexhaustible supply of optimism. They knew that looking in the right places - places where the geological conditions suggested gold *might* be found - made a lot more sense than just looking *anywhere*. The odds were still long, but a modicum of planning and common sense made a lot of difference - if they were lucky, the difference between success and failure.

Someone said '*success begins when you acquire the habit of hard work.*' Prospecting *is* hard work, and, without seriously applying yourself to it, literally nothing will happen!

If the idea of income appeals to you as a continuous process, prospecting must be a continuous process too. Q.E.D!

*Prospecting is like breathing - it must be a lifetime habit. And, like breathing, it only becomes a problem when it ceases to be a habit!*

We are all surrounded by millions of people who have a need for our product or service. You could walk through your home town from one end to the other and you would rub shoulders with thousands of people. The problem lies in getting any one of them to sit down in a one-to-one situation, and to be able to talk to them.

In your daily life, opportunities to talk to people occur all the time, especially if you happen to be a gregarious person. It is only a question of always being alert as you seek conversational opportunities. But that is very opportunist - and a pretty haphazard way of prospecting. Things must be a great deal better organised than that! Unless prospecting is well-organised under a planned system it can become little better than a series of hit-and-miss thrusts. It is not unlike trying to shoot down a plane with an old fashioned anti-aircraft gun. As we have all seen in wartime movies, the result is a lot of puffs of smoke from exploding shells all around the aircraft, with rarely a direct hit. The weapon employed today would be the heat-seeking missile which can, once it has been programmed with the necessary information, sense and identify its target, lock on to it, and guarantee the direct hit.

Prospecting must be like that! On target to guarantee a high possibility of success. Good planning and research are needed since the more you know about your prospect, the better your chances of eventual success - making a sale - will be.

Quite clearly, this will be determined by your ability to prospect and see a sufficient number of the right people at the right time. I have never like referring to selling as a numbers game, and yet, really and truly, that is exactly what it is. It has been said that even a bad salesman will succeed -

relatively speaking - providing he sees a sufficient number of people. Similarly, the person who is technically skilled and may even be a brilliant exponent of selling, can only prosper providing he always has a constant flow of prospects.

Successful sales people are often looked on as lucky. It is odd though, don't you think, that the more people they see, the luckier they seem to become? If that is luck, it is also very closely related to prospecting, for without prospects, all the luck in the world won't make for success - so, let's take a look at a number of methods of gathering the information we might need to create a list of prospective customers. Some of these thoughts will not be appropriate within the context of some forms of selling. Obviously not everyone works - or is required to work - in the same way. As with all things in life, be selective - use the things that will work for you - *take the cream and leave the milk!*

● *Occupational prospects.* That is to say, names of people or companies engaged in a particular business or industry. These would usually be found in trade directories, yellow pages etc.

● *Generated leads.* Leads coming from advertising, inviting the completion of a coupon, or the making of a phone call.

● *Visual prospecting.* Simply the result of keeping your eyes open and making notes of what you see.

● *Casual prospecting.* The result of unplanned or spontaneous conversational approaches.

- **Mailshots.** Of course, the names and addresses have to be researched first, but this can be a way of generating a lot of leads, depending on the quality of the approach.

- **Telephone prospecting.** This is often done by professional *telesales* girls - but the only object of the call is to arrange an appointment.

- **Cold calling.** Domestic door-knocking is not very professional and comes close to being viewed as an invasion of privacy. Cold calling on businesses, however, is a very different matter.

- **Referred leads.** These, as we know, are gold dust. They are the most solid prospects of all as the names are generated through personal recommendation.

There then, are a few of the most common ways of getting in front of people to enable you to tell your story. It might be worth taking each one of the headings in turn to put a little more flesh on the bare bones. Remember that, whatever the method of prospecting, planning and research are the keynotes of the operation. It can take longer to put together a telephone list than it takes to ring the names on it, so, if one is able to *qualify* those names as well as possible, to cut out the dross of wasted time and effort, the chances of success will be so much higher.

### Occupational prospects.

The obvious sources are, as I have said, trade directories and yellow pages. All the methods of prospecting I have suggested overlap one another. Occupational prospects could be the result of cruising around industrial estates, gathering names for future approaches, either by telephone or letter. It is easy, in doing this, to qualify the prospect to a reasonable extent by stopping for a moment to call at the reception desk to collect a compliments slip. Get the girl on the desk to give you the name of the person you will need to see. You may want to write or telephone, or, at a later date you might choose to make your approach by means of another cold call. It might even be possible to see your man there and then - but that would depend on how defensive the receptionist might be!

It is far better to be armed with the name of the person you wish to meet, when cold calling. A bit of time spent in information gathering will always pay off. For example, if his name is John Smith, ask for him as *John Smith* as it somehow implies that you already know him. Asking simply to see Mr.Smith will probably cause all the expected difficulties. Remember, you are not the only person who tries to see John Smith! A company receptionist is often instructed to act as the first line of defence. It is important that you get past this initial hurdle so, if you display total confidence and allow it to be assumed that you already know the person you are asking to see, your chances of getting your way are that much better.

### General leads

These are of the greatest value. If a company has gone to the expense of an advertising campaign, inviting potential customers to respond by filling in a coupon or some other response mechanism, the leads must not be wasted. There are many sales managers who take the line that such leads are only given to the best salesmen - they should never be used as crutches for the poor performer.

Leads of this sort should, in theory, always be converted into business. What could be better than to visit people or businesses who have actually invited you to come and see them?

## *Visual prospecting*

It is amazing what you notice when you keep your eyes open. Clearly, it depends very much what branch of sales you are in as to how much visual prospecting can help you. Just consider, for a moment, the number of tradesman's vans you see as you travel about - all with a name and at least a telephone number, if not a complete address.

We have already covered industrial estates and the amount of information that can be gathered visually. Again, it depends who you are looking for, but the cards in newsagents' shop windows can be a great source of local self-employed people offering an amazing variety of services.

Local newspapers are a fund of information to certain selling professions - not just the advertising , but the stories of local interest.

## *Casual prospecting*

This can only be left to the individual's imagination and initiative. It is really no more that listening, watching and generally being alert to what is happening all around you.

## *Mailshots*

Often used, like other forms of advertising, to generate leads for a sales force, a good mailshot has the advantage of being able to pinpoint a specific area, income group, social group, age group, etc. It is really *qualified advertising* and lead generation, and the resultant leads can be of great value.

The use of mailshots, however, is very much a numbers game since an average return of around 2% to 3% is regarded as being quite good. But that 2% can represent a lot of potential buyers - if the exercise is carried out on a sufficiently large scale.

Just as when seeking an appointment on the telephone, one should not say too much about the product, it is not *always* a good idea to include product literature with a mailshot. One of the purposes of the mailing can be to get to see the targetted person to enable a personal approach in a planned and organised manner. Providing *too* much information about the product *too* soon is simply giving the prospective customer every opportunity to reject it before there has been any opportunity for *need* to be established and revealed through fact-finding, and indeed, the whole process of Four-Square-Selling .

There is a psychology related to the construction of a mailshot that is interesting. Every paragraph should, ideally, be putting across the central message in some way, since people have a way of reading selected bits of an unsolicited letter or leaflet. Most of us will almost certainly start by looking at any PS the letter may contain. Next we will look at the signature, and then the majority of us will start reading somewhere around the middle of the letter - and, if it interests us, eventually go back to the beginning.

On that basis it will be appreciated that any PS the letter may contain is important as a *first* message, and, as such, should stick in the memory. There was a business man in the north of England who used to produce a classic mailshot letter. Before it was sent out, it was crumpled into a ball and then roughly smoothed out again before being properly folded and put into its envelope. The letter contained a PS which read...*'this letter has been pre-crumpled for your convenience.'* A day or two after the letters had been posted, the sender would telephone the recipients and give his name. After allowing for the expected silence that greeted this information he would say...*'I am the person who sent you the pre-crumpled letter.'* This was usually greeted with such amusement that the conversation was off to a flying start! That man's expected return from mailshots was greatly in excess of the normal 2% - but, as you might imagine, the way it was handled relied very much on the personality of the man who was able to carry it off.

### Telephone prospecting

We have probably all suffered from this at some time! The double glazing, home improvements and kitchen salesmen rely very much on cold telephone contacting - either handled by themselves or by girls who do cold telephoning all the time, working either on a fixed fee basis or receiving a commission on the sales that result from the appointments they acquire for the salesman.

Some people are very good indeed at cold telephoning whilst the majority are pretty bad, falling back all too often on the old chestnuts such as ...*'our designer is working in your area next week...'* This always reminds me of men who knock on doors towards the end of a day and claim to have a load of tar macadam left over from a job they have just completed near by. Your driveway could be transformed in no time at all - and at very little cost if they could come and do the job whilst they are still in the area.

### Cold calling

Its particular appeal - for those to whom it does appeal - lies in the fact that cold calling is totally unpredictable.

115

There is an unknown quality about it.   It represents the excitement of the chase,  of not knowing what lies round the next corner!

We are talking,  of course, about cold calling on businesses.   I have never liked the idea of domestic cold calling.   There are people who can get away with it,  of that I have no dopubt,      but no matter how it is handled,  you cannot get away from the fact that it represents an invasion of personal privacy,  and that is something of which  people have become very aware.

There are times when prospecting activities are flagging.   It is at times like this when a day of cold calling on businesses, ideally in an area new to the salesman, can provide a tremendous motivational boost.   Such a day - for the person who can do it (and enjoy it!) - can produce so many new and exciting leads and so much potential business that it could take a week or two to follow everything through to a conclusion.

### Referred leads
Another source of true gold.   It is a strange thing,  but many salesmen find it extremely difficult to ask for referred leads. Once again,  this is probably yet another manifestation of the fear of rejection.

It is also strange that, on being asked,  most customers seem to suddenly suffer a severe mental block!   This,  of course,  may be because they do not want to give you any information.    It can also be - and this is the more likely reason - that, on being confronted with the situation,  they have no real starting point to trigger a mental process.   The simple question *'Who do you know who...?'*  is the best possible prompt - and you can literally add anything at all on

**116**

to the end of that question.  For example, going back to our earlier example of a sales conversation, *'Mr.Smith, who do you know who has a lot of grass to cut?'*

If you have established a good relationship with your new customer, the interesting thing about referred leads is that any you get will be to people remarkably like the person who provided them.  People tend to associate with individuals very much like themselves - usually in the same income bracket and with similar social trappings and commitments.

I met a young and successful salesman years ago who claimed that he had never made a cold call in his life.  He started with a lead from his company and obtained referred leads from almost everyone he dealt with so that he had a prospect list that just kept on growing.  He insisted that there are certain rules one should follow in building a customer bank in this way.  The first was that you always ask if you may use the name of the person who gave you the lead.  The second is that you always let that person know the outcome (but obviously not the details) of your approach.  This, he claimed, very often lead to being given more leads.

It is difficult to write about prospecting in a way that is appropriate to everyone engaged in selling.  Many salesmen might never have to do their own prospecting, yet I think it is true to say that most commission earning - as opposed to salaried - salesmen will be expected to generate at least some of their new business.  Prospecting, too, will vary so much from one industry to another to the extent that methods that are fine for one would be totally inappropriate to another.

Prospecting is not just something that must be actively pursued in the early stages of a sales career.  It must be an on-going process at all times, simply to keep up the supply of new contacts that will be important to your pattern of business.

In the normal course of a developing career, evolving a work pattern is vital to eventual success. I have devised a system which, if followed to the letter, will guarantee success in the shortest possible time from completely new beginnings.

Everything in this book follows a pattern of *fours*, and the system I am about to outline is no exception - *The Four Day Week plan.*

# 10
## *The Four-Day-Week Plan*

There are some things in life that, when presented to one, seem too good to be true - and that is usually the reason for doing precisely nothing about them!

Human nature is such that there is always that little demon sitting on one's shoulder saying *'well if it's so damned good, why isn't everyone doing it?'* Most propositions that fall into the too-good-to-be-true category need to be seriously examined since it is more than likely they will call for either total commitment or sheer hard work - quite possibly both.

As I have already mentioned, the idea I am about to pass on to you works without a shadow of a doubt. But it only works for those prepared to work for *it*.

The simple proposition is this - *does the idea of only working four days a week appeal to you?* We are talking of a very specifically organised working week, and the first few weeks required to set it in motion will involve sheer hard labour - that is where the commitment comes in. At the end of this initial period you will have organised and established an income pattern that will keep the orders, sales and payments coming in in a most comforting way. You will never be short of work, and never again be short of prospects.

Committing yourself to such a plan is no more than a short-term inconvenience in exchange for long-term stability and success. Not a great price to pay, is it?

One thing I should point out is that this plan cannot possibly be of use to everyone in selling. It is ideally designed for the self-employed, commission-earning salesman - but it may be possible to tailor it to people who do not exactly fit that description - that I can only leave to the individual.

So, how does the concept appeal? Of course you haven't been told what must be done yet but, remember, *telling is not selling!* Before the scheme is revealed to you, it is important that you recognise you have a *need* for it - a need for a well-organised working plan that can even incorporate leisure pursuits, and yet still give you the best part of three days off out of each seven. Too good to be true? Not at all! - just read on...

Many people spend far too much time chasing around in a disorganised way, believing themselves to be *busy* and yet, in reality mistaking their busy-ness for *activity*. There is a world of difference between those two words.

Try answering these questions:
● If you had just two good selling appointments each morning, and two more each afternoon, wouldn't you feel life was quite pleasant?
● ...and if that pattern was reproduced each day, Monday to Thursday, wouldn't you find that rather agreeable?
● ...and if those 16 selling appointments during your four-day-week were organised into a sensible geographical pattern, wouldn't that make a lot of sense too?
● ...and, if you had time for a round of golf during your four working days - or for anything else you might like to do on a regular basis, wouldn't life seem very civilised indeed?

Well, if you like the sound of that, you have accepted the Four-day-week-Plan! Do I hear moans and groans? Setting up 16 appointments a week is, I accept, a monumental task. But that is the challenge and commitment you must be prepared to accept because - *the first week of the plan is the only time you will have to do it!*

After that first week, providing you did actually start off with 16 genuine appointments, which could easily have taken you a week to set up, I promise you, you will be into a rhythm of work that will cause you to get out of bed in the morning full of anticipation, eager to get started! This is how it works...

### Set up your diary for WEEK 1

The shaded areas in the diagram below represent appointment times that must be filled - in the case of the first week, that means all 16 . The symbols at the right hand side of an appointment panel show the outcome of the interview...

● = a sale. RL = referred lead

| | | | | |
|---|---|---|---|---|
| **Mon AM** | 9.00 | | 11.30 | |
| **PM** | 2.00 | ● | 3.30 | RL |
| **Tues AM** | 9.00 | RL | 11.30 | |
| **PM** | 2.00 | | 3.30 | ● |
| **Wed AM** | 9.00 | ● | 11.30 | RL |
| **PM** | 2.00 | | 3.30 | RL |
| **Thur AM** | 9.00 | RL | 11.30 | |
| **PM** | 2.00 | ● | 3.30 | |

These will all be new, first-time appointments - and, as you can see above, the first week resulted in four sales and five referred leads. That is about par for the course from 16 good appointments.

It is important to schedule in leisure time as the first entry in the diary, even before working appointments are booked. This ensures that there *is* leisure time built into the working week and that it is not left to chance - a sure way of it never happening!

Suppose then that a leisure period has been put in on Wednesday. If the first morning appointment was put into the diary for 8.30 (instead of 9.00), and the second was scheduled for 10.00 (instead of 11.30), then the first PM appointment was made for 3.00 (instead of 2.00), and the second for 5.30 (instead of 3.30), ample time would have been planned into that day to accommodate a game of golf or a sailing lesson - or whatever takes your fancy.

For salesmen who can work in the evenings, the flexibility is obviously even greater - always providing that the pattern of 4 appointments per day is maintained, for that is crucial to the plan. And it is just as important that *no more than 4 appointments are made for each day.*

As we have seen, the outcome of that first week was four sales. It is reasonable to assume that another 4 of the first week's appointments will require a second visit before a sale takes place.

So, the pattern for week two is already becoming more encouraging. Four of the appointment times will be taken up with second calls, and a further five should be taken up by contacts made with the referred leads. That only leaves 7 appointments to fill from stone cold prospecting. When do you think this is going to be done? *Friday* of course!

Now *that* does not negate the four-day-week idea. Remember, we are still only in the early stages, setting up the ultimate scheme. Think of Friday as the day when, after the diary is set up for next week, you can take the rest of the day off. In the early weeks, Friday will be fairly active but, as the plan progresses, you will reach a point when only 2 or 3 first-time appointments have to be made, so most of the day will be free.

So now, let's look at week 2 of the Plan..

## WEEK 2

| | | | |
|---|---|---|---|
| **Mon AM** | 9.00 ● 2nd | 11.30 2nd | |
| **PM** | 2.00 RL 2nd | 3.30 RL | |
| **Tues AM** | 9.00 2nd 3rd | 11.30 RL ● | |
| **PM** | 2.00 RL | 3.30 2nd | |
| **Wed AM** | 9.00 RL RL ● | 11.30 2nd RL ● | |
| **PM** | 2.00 ● | 3.30 RL | |
| **Thur AM** | 9.00 RL 2nd | 11.30 RL 2nd | |
| **PM** | 2.00 2nd | 3.30 2nd | |

The shaded areas above represent the 4 second appointments (2nd - shown after the appointment time at the left of the panel), and five appointments from referred leads (RL). So, in week 2 there are only 7 new appointments (the white spaces) to fill. Already the task is becoming easier!

In Week 2 let's assume 5 sales (see results at right hand side of each appointment panel). Two came from Referred Leads

(Tuesday 11.30 and Wednesday 9.00), two were from new first appointments (Monday 9.00 and Wednesday 2.00), and one was from a 2nd appointment with someone originally seen in Week 1(Wednesday 11.30).

The work that has to be done on Friday is already becoming easier. In Week 2 we collected referred leads from 5 sources, we made 6 x 2nd appointments for Week 3, one of which is an almost certain sale since it was made after a successful sale (Monday 9.00). So the commitment for Friday of Week 2 is to get 4 new appointments - and that should not take long at all with a good prospect list. So...

## WEEK 3.

| Mon AM | 9.00          2nd | 11.30 RL |
|---|---|---|
| PM | 2.00 RL          RL ● | 3.30 2nd |
| Tues AM | 9.00 RL | 11.30          ● |
| PM | 2.00 2nd | 3.30 2nd |
| Wed AM | 9.00          RL | 11.30 RL          ● |
| PM | 2.00 3rd          ●● | 3.30 RL          2nd |
| Thur AM | 9.00 2nd | 11.30          2nd |
| PM | 2.00 RL          ● | 3.30 2nd          RL |

...and so it goes on! Week after week there is the satisfaction of continuity, the satisfying feeling each Monday, instead of that awful *what am I going to do* feeling, of knowing that there is a full week ahead - a week of real opportunity.

Of course, as time passes, the weeks fill up even quicker because there will be a flow of sure-fire appointments coming from the Hot Box and the Month Box, as customers need to be contacted anew. Maybe, in your line of business, anniversaries have some significance, or maybe service calls are part of the pattern.

Let me emphasise the point again -

*...if you follow the Four-Day-Week Plan, you will not only succeed, but you will do so in half the time it would take without such a plan.*

**It may look too good to be true, but it isn't.**
**All you have to do is believe in it but, above all,**

**believe in YOURSELF!**

# 11

# *The High-Flyer and the Wealth Syndrome*

Salesmen are by nature competitive people.  In this lurks both an advantage and a danger.  It is the competitive element that will motivate the salesman to greater effort,  for  the thing he enjoys most of all is recognition - public recognition - and especially  the recognition of his peers.     The  salesman  is an achiever and a goal-setter,  but only providing his efforts and achievements are constantly recognised.

Most sales organisations take advantage of the naturally competitive nature of its sales staff and employ this factor  to their own benefit by a system of motivation through, not just recognition,  but something more obviously tangible as well - financial reward,  or benefit in kind.

A man/woman-of-the-month award,  monetary and other prizes,  and of course,  the ultimate accolade,  a place on the annual overseas sales convention planned to take place in some exotic venue.

All these forms of performance-related recognition and reward will drive the high achiever further up the performance and earnings table.    This then is the heady world of the high-flyer - *but beware!* - because it is not always such an enviable state as one might imagine.

Constant achievement produces its own pressures, stresses and demands.    To constantly occupy that high earnings platform produces all manner of anxieties.   As we have seen, everyone enjoys reward and the public recognition that accompanies it. In exactly the same way, nobody enjoys being seen to fail.

Now failure is a purely relative thing. To the high achiever, failure may be no more than *just missing* a target and being pushed into second place by a rival. The fact that the target he missed would have been way beyond the achievement of many of his peers is irrelevant. It is staying in the No.1 position, to the high-flyer, that is so vitally important. His achievement has little to do with earnings - he is accustomed to those rewards - indeed, he has probably created a life-style to accommodate them - it is *status* that is the supremely important factor. It is for this reason that a very curious situation can, and all too often does arise...

## THE WEALTH SYNDROME

Let's take a look at the psychology of achievement, reward and recognition. People, surprisingly perhaps, are *not* motivated by money - unless, of course, they simply do not have any. Assuming a reasonable level of earnings, the driving force or motivation is recognition, as we have already seen.

Once a salesman gets used to a reasonable level of earnings, one of two things can happen. The first option is that he will drop into a comfort zone of his own devising where he can relax contentedly. He may see no point in striving for anything better because he is better off than he has ever been before. But there is an alternative - he will be excited by his achievement and the recognition it has brought him, and be motivated by that to raise his sights and move a little further up the earnings ladder to establish another, slightly better comfort zone into which he may happily drop.

He may, however, at this point, begin to realise that by establishing and setting himself goals - and it is important that these are set by *him* and not by anyone else - he can achieve anything on which he sets his sights.

Now he is beginning to be driven very much by peer-recognition, and greatly enjoying the status this brings. His earnings naturally are directly related to his achievements and so he is improving his life-style and beginning to surround himself with the financial commitments that are implicit to his new-found affluence.

The adulation he enjoys through the recognition his achievements bring becomes a heady cocktail and affects him almost like a drug. As with most habitual stimulants, he begins to feel this is something he cannot do without - and here lurks the real danger, for *the wealth syndrome* is now at work.

Fear of failure, or, more precisely, *fear of being seen to fail*, can become a real problem to some people. Anyone who has spent any time in the sales world will have seen this syndrome at work. It can drive a successful person into devious and dishonest practices, producing behaviour of a sort that is totally unnecessary, simply in order to stay in the No.1 position on the sales ladder. There is no need for extra money *but there is a real and deep-seated fear of being seen as a failure by their peers* - and yet it is so often the behaviour they employ to avoid this that is the instrument of their eventual destruction through these strained and unnatural circumstances.

A sort of fanaticism blinds and drives them, quite irrationally, to do things that they must *know* cannot possibly go undetected. But fanaticism is a strange bedfellow. It has been described as *doubling your efforts after you have lost sight of your aims.* In the world of high earnings, the possibility for an erosion of both values and ethics is always present, but so long as any individual is aware of the dangers, - and aware of what it is that drives them towards these dangers - they have every chance of avoiding the trap and enjoying the fruits of their own success to the full.

I would like to believe that anyone who follows the practices of *Four-Square-Selling* will be virtually immune to falling into the trap that *The Wealth Syndrome* represents. Once good work practices are learned and have, by constant application, become habitual, the on-going sales experience would be so sound that there literally would be no possible reason for any form of devious practice, since success too would have become the norm.

# 12
# *Random thoughts...*

## SALES RHYTHM

The skilled exponent of selling will understand this expression only too well.   During the course of the sales cycle,  assuming the salesman is really skilled in both product knowledge and,  even more importantly,  *people* knowledge - the two corner stones of his profession - something fascinating begins to happen.   It is a manifestation I call *sales rhythm*.   It is the product of professionalism coupled with a good understanding of people and the ways in which they can behave.   As a state of empathy develops between salesman and potential customer,   this rhythm begins to grow which dictates the directional flow of conversation and interest.

It is very difficult for two salesmen to work together since every individual,  once some degree of experience has been acquired, develops a way of thinking and working which is very personal, following logical patterns which unfold as the relationship between seller and buyer expands.

No two people will think in the same way and the difficulty,  when attempting to work together,  is that one person can so easily disturb the thinking pattern of the other.

Anyone who is successful in sales will have certainly developed a style which is very much his own. *Four-Square-Selling* often involves asking questions that are necessary to establish an idea in the customer's mind.   Each question is very much related to the answers to the previous question,   so that a directional theme evolves.   The conversation has to be conducted in a very relaxed and casual way.   No two salesmen will conduct a conversation of this sort in the same way. Whilst one is busy developing his theme, it is easy for the other to become impatient, not appreciating the direction his companion is taking. He can so easily upset the rhythm by throwing in questions and observations calculated to enliven the proceedings. *But such questions may be ones for which· the customer is not yet prepared.* The customer can be distracted all too easily from the flow that is leading towards a conclusion satisfactory to both him and the salesman.

## ONE MORE WARNING!

As skills develop and selling experience is gained, one begins to realise how easy it is to influence others by the use of emotive language, even quite innocently, in one's natural enthusiasm. Remembering what we have already discussed regarding manipulation and motivation, there is a real case for being aware of one's selling power so as not to allow it to get out of hand. There are occasions when the brakes need to be applied a little because one's influence over the other person is developing too strongly. Always be aware of the possibility of unintentional manipulation.

## SALES MANAGEMENT

The people that are attracted to a career in sales are, in the main, essentially free spirits, perceiving the profession as one in which they can range freely, controlling themselves to a large extent. They are people who live life on their toes, alert to the opportunities of the moment and very much reliant on their own skills, abilities and instincts. Apart from the need for some sort of formalised training, sales people are of the type that doesn't mind being told what to do, but objects very strongly to being told *how to do it.*

A good sales manager will recognise all these things and see them as advantages. Hopefully, he will have done the salesman's job before moving into management at any level, so will appreciate exactly what is involved. It is unlikely that a sales manager who has not actually experienced selling in the field first hand - and there are quite a few managers at all levels that have not - will be very good at his job.

The good salesman is such a unique creature, and needs so much understanding, that the manager who has *been there* himself will always be the person to get the most out of his sales team. He will know, for example, that it is useless ranting and raving about sales figures and the need for greater production - remember *telling is not selling!* - but will be aware of the value of delegation.

Delegation is the assignment of responsibility. The sales manager is responsible for a team which is expected to produce a certain level of production. His job then, is to delegate the responsibility for achieving these targets throughout his sales team. Delegation must never be seen as a diminution of power or the relinquishing of control - it is merely the assignation of a degree of responsibility.

In accepting responsibility, the salesman is, in effect, being told what to do. *How to do it* is then down to him - making the decisions which the acceptance of responsibility demand of him. The good manager is well aware of this and sees his own role as maintaining the feel-good-factor within his team. He will be well aware also of that odd phenomenon that affects all of life in various ways, the 80/20 rule (known as Parato's Law), operating within his team - 80% of the production will be achieved by 20% of the team.

The obvious question is *what are the 20% doing that the 80% aren't?* The answer, most likely, is that they are caring about people, not just looking for sales. They are seeing their prospective customers as people who might benefit from a product or service which will add value to their lives. In other words, they are approaching the sales situation with the right attitudes.

Another aspect of this inescapable phenomenon is that, in their daily lives, most people produce 80% of their work through a mere 20% of their effort. The question here is, *what are they doing with the remaining 80% of their day?* Chasing their tails, doing things that are not of any great importance - mistaking being *busy* for being *active.* More stress is caused by chasing after unnecessary things than by doing the things that are productive and rewarding.

All this adds up to a simple formula - identify the things in your working day that comprise the 20% *and concentrate on doing them even more efficiently.*

### Take the cream and leave the milk!

Life will become easier, you will do less but accomplish more, and the stress level will decrease. Stress has no place in the context of selling. Over anxiety and nervousness are very easily transmitted, and once they touch your customer, the sale is not going to happen. There is a Chinese saying:

### 'When the water is up to your chin, even a ripple can drown you'

Remember, the things we concentrate on are the things that actually happen.

No matter how successful a salesman is, his need for praise and recognition never dies. It is the manager's job to see that this all-important factor is delivered and is never neglected. The high-flyers in a sales team are, of course, the 20%. They are important - but no more than the other 80%, for some of *them* will become part of the 20%, given time and the right sort of encouragement.     The 80/20 rule can be observed operating at all levels throughout any corporate body, right from head office, down through regional sales offices to the branch offices.     When one considers the 80%, within this broader spectrum, one cannot fail to be impressed by the fact that they are the true backbone of the company and the sales force, producing the plodding statistical averages necessary to the continuance of any business.     The high-flyers can be relied to go on producing their pyrotechnics - the rockets that shoot for the stars, but also have the potential to fizzle out and fall back to earth, spent and useless.

The ground occupied by the great 80% will always be the training ground for the future 20%.   Everyone needs constant attention and encouragement - the example of *leadership by beckoning, not by pointing* is what the good sales manager will provide.

A happy sales team will be a productive sales team.   All attitudes in any organisation emanate from the top and feed downwards - and that applies just as much to bad attitudes as to good ones.   The attitudes of a manager will be reflected through his sales team and their performance.    In just the same way, the attitudes that feed down from a head office will be reflected throughout that company at every level.   All too often,    simple facts like that tend to get forgotten, sometimes quite conveniently when the question of apportioning blame for poor performance is raised.

## WHO MOTIVATES THE MOTIVATOR?

It is easy to overlook the fact that everyone, at all levels throughout a company - and particularly throughout a sales organisation - has the same basic needs for recognition. That pat on the back, recognition of a task well done, must never be forgotten - and yet, all too frequently *it is forgotten*. People, in all manner of jobs, will perform their tasks better for the boss who always shows an awareness of them and the work they do.

### *Disregard employees at your peril!*

But everyone in a large organisation has someone to whom they report - and that person should fulfil the role of motivator to those for whom he is responsible. The chain of motivation and recognition is clearly visible and yet so often distorted or corroded by familiarity. It is so easy to forget the simplest things in life - those fundamental human requirements that mean so much to every one of us.

There has been a great deal of discussion in the media regarding what is described as bullying in the work place. If this exists to the degree that has been suggested, it must be a thoroughly destructive and counter-productive force adversely affecting every aspect of a companies potential. People cannot possible be motivated through fear, and anyone, at any level of management who attempts to dominate those responsible to him or her, is simply digging their own eventual grave. The result will be poor, if not totally indifferent performance, negativism, bad attendance through stress-related illness, and a complete loss of involvement in the company's interests.

Companies should declare a policy, in their own best interests to stamp out any form of bullying in the workplace.

136

It is not in the interests of any company to employ anyone demonstrating such a total lack of human understanding that they mistake the stick for the carrot as a motivational tool.

So, the sales manager needs as much motivation and recognition as the people under him receive from him. He functions very much in isolation, as any leader does, and so sympathetic contact from superiors is very important to his performance, and through him, to the performance of his team. Unfortunately, the successful manager, just as the successful salesman, very often suffers from the neglect that comes from familiarity - the expectation that, *because he has always been successful, he will continue to be successful.*

This is simply not so. Once the manager or the salesman begins to suspect neglect or disinterest from superiors, his performance suffers. If the lack of love and recognition goes on too long, he may even begin to peer over other people's garden walls to see whether the grass is greener.

All levels of management, then, are sales jobs in the widest meaning of the word. People who understand the sales process - *Four-Square-Selling* - will usually make good managers. Management is, after all, no more than selling your ideas to other people, often to the people who are going to have to implement them. Every innovative idea must be sold. Small, routine matters can be dealt with by instruction, more important matters are selling events.

To create a scenario to emphasise the importance of *selling* in the managerial context, take a large company whose sales figures have slumped. The directors, being under pressure from their chairman and the shareholders decide to call a meeting of all the company's sales managers.

The situation is critical as the directors realise their own positions are threatened by the situation unless they come up with the solution - increased sales.

The meeting is convened very quickly and the venue is the usual large conference hotel. Because of the situation that has lead to the down-turn in sales, the morale of the sales force does not stand very high, so the audience is both curious and apprehensive over the reasons for this meeting being called at such short notice.

There are two courses of action the managing director can take - to put all his cards on the table and seek the understanding and co-operation of the sales managers, or to blame them for the company's poor performance and attempt to set the matter right by threats.

The first route is *the selling route,* whilst the alternative is the *telling route.* Unfortunately, perhaps in his anxiety and the need for immediate improvement, he chooses the wrong route and, rather than dangle the carrot, wields the big stick as his way of motivating the flagging situation.

All this achieves is to antagonise the managers and create an atmosphere of deep resentment. Seeing he is getting no response whatsoever, the managing director wades further into the mire by telling his audience, very forcibly, that they should realise they have the finest leadership team in him and his co-directors of any company in the industry, and anyone who doesn't accept that has no place in the scheme of things.

Handled with a well thought out sales approach, such a meeting could have ended on a motivational high, sending the sales managers back to their teams feeling there was a new challenge to be met, and the situation would have already been on the brink of transformation. Instead, the outcome could now be a spate of resignations as sales managers seek other, more sympathetic employers who will appreciate them and show them the respect and recognition they feel they deserve.

## SELF LIMITATIONS
*It has always been far easier to fail than to succeed!*

Human beings have a way of placing obstacles in their own path, imposing limitations that persuade them that something cannot be done.

In India elephants are trained to believe that a three foot iron stake stuck in the ground can hold them. When the animal is very young it is tethered to such a stake, against which it is allowed to struggle for several days. Eventually the young elephant realises that it cannot get away. An elephant never forgets, and it is that fact that will tether a full-grown animal who is, in reality, quite capable of pulling the stake out of the ground almost without noticing. The animal is imprisoned by its own lack of imagination.

Some people will complain that they have difficulty in getting through to others. *So long as they believe this, they never will.* Their belief in their own capabilities needs to be strengthened. It is only like the assumption that *closing a sale* is fraught with difficulties and needs special techniques to bring the sale to a conclusion. As soon as people truly believe they can do a thing, they will do it.

I took as the title to my last book ('Believe you can!') part of a quotation from the industrialist Henry Ford. He said '*if you believe you can do a thing, or you believe you cannot, you are right.*' If we go on erecting our own barriers, the outcome will always be the same.

There is a particular type of barrier that we all suffer or benefit from, as the case may be, and that is what I call *The Delay Syndrome*. There are, in the course of a working year, many barriers that seem to be regarded as having some special significance. These include Christmas, Easter and all Bank Holidays. They are not actual blocks to achievement in themselves - the problem is their influence that extends to at least a week before the actual date, and often too, for a few days afterwards.

Christmas is an occasion that justifies delay by stopping normal working life for a few days, but a national habit has developed whereby Easter and every other public holiday have also become natural and legitimate blockages. *Leave it until after the holiday*, is the common cry which begins to be heard a good week before all Bank Holidays. Why should these events be regarded as traffic stoppers? The wasted time nationally must be astronomic.

## SALES SCRIPTS

In writing that heading, I was tempted to add - *forget them!* But that would upset a lot of people. There are many sales managers who would not like the suggestion that sales scripts are for parrots and therefore not generally very professional. They might argue that the majority of their salesmen could not operate without a script. If this really is the case perhaps they should look at their recruiting and selection methods - it could be that they are working with poor basic material.

Maybe these are dangerous remarks to be making, but quite frankly, I have heard so many poor scripts, badly performed, that I would prefer to encourage anyone who thinks selling is for him, to find his own words to express his own feelings. People cannot always be forced into moulds devised by others in the expectation that they will perform to a standard which may not be easy or natural to them.

The *Four-Square-Selling* system provides a track on which to run - a series of natural prompts to keep one on course, providing reminders of what needs to be said at any given point in the sales sequence. It is *not* a rigid discipline, indeed it can absorb all the flexibility anyone could wish.

Salesmen are actors! They need to be able to get into the shoes of their customer to understand how he feels. But unlike the professional actor, they are rarely capable of using a sales script in a way that sounds completely natural and unrehearsed. A script is a blanket technique - the resort of the insecure - but insecure people will never become good sales people.

Selling requires confidence, spontaneity and a degree of courage, even bravery. It calls for a high level of self-belief, not to say self-esteem. With the right track to run on, the right person will find the right things to say.

Scripts after long and constant use begin to lose their meaning to the person who is reliant upon them. The content, through familiarity and the boredom that comes from the sound of one's own voice saying the same old things, becomes eroded by the constant repetition, corners tend to be cut and things are liable to get left out. We have probably all experienced the scripted performance which, if interrupted, throws the performer into confusion, often necessitating a return to the script at the point before the interruption took place.

Providing you have recognised the *style* of person you are speaking to, you should find you can relate and respond to them in a perfectly natural way.

## WOMEN AND SELLING

I have always had the greatest respect for women in the sales situation. They can be extremely good, and, as with so many examples of women working in what has often been regarded as a man's world, they feel a need to be even better than their male counterparts.

They have so much going for them - not least of all their femininity - but they must always be aware of the power of that particular asset, as it can work both for or against them unless it is properly controlled.

Women are usually very good at making appointments - and this is the area where femininity can be a great help. There are many successful salesmen who employ girls to make their appointments for them, and we have all probably experienced 'tele-sales' girls.

Clearly a woman must take care not to play on the male/female aspect of relationships too much. Simply being a woman, and coming across on the telephone as an attractive personality, will easily secure the appointment, especially with men. I see nothing wrong with this - providing that from the moment she arrives for the appointment, she behaves in such a *professional and business-like manner* that any other ideas that might have been entertained, go out of the window. She *must* establish complete control of the conversation and the occasion *immediately* - but without being so dominant as to dent a male ego!

Many women have had great success in the sales field. They instinctively understand how to use their natural charm, rarely overstep the mark, and establish excellent relationships that are of immense value to those who employ them. They are professional, ethical and reliable. If they have any real problem it is that of *rejection.*

Women are less resilient than men in this respect and are inclined to take rejection in a very personal way. This is quite understandable, and once they have learned that rejection is mostly related to the job or the product, and not to the individual, they can usually come to terms with it.

## SUCCESS & FAILURE

*Failure is not just falling down.*
*It is rather, having fallen down, not having the wit,*
*guts or determination to get up and start again.*

If you are successful, it is important to recognise *why* you are successful. If you notice that by doing certain things habitually, you are successful, **keep on doing them!** Do not try to reinvent the wheel. Keep doing the things that work.

It is so much easier to acquire the habit of failure than the habit of success. Some people develop a habit of always looking for the down-side in any situation. If there isn't one there, it is all too easy to create one.

We have all met people for whom nothing ever seems to go right. They have developed the habit of believing that nothing ever works out for them - *and so things don't.* Fortunes have been made by people sticking to acquired habits and by doing things in a certain way. Fortunes have also been lost by people tiring of habitual, but successful routine, and being tempted to try doing things in a different way.

If you are a success at selling, it will almost certainly be because you are *concerned about people*, and not just preoccupied with the *idea* of selling. Remember, *you are a decision getter,* not simply a salesman. Your job is talking

**143**

to people with the sole aim of *getting them to make decisions that they are happy to make*. The result is, of course, a sale - but a sale attended by all the right feelings.

Buying and selling are no more than an interchange between people. Your success will come by helping others to get what they want, not through just doing what *you* want.

## INDECISION & NEGATIVISM

Indecision is mental paralysis. It is the great thief of opportunity, productivity and happiness. Learn by determination to make decisions quickly and to stick by them. Any decision must be implemented by massive action.

*Decision determines your direction*
*- action takes you to your goal.*

Negativism is a terrible stumbling block to success and achievement. It is like an infection and can so easily be passed from one person to another. Avoid the company of negative people for surely they will eventually infect you and drag you down to their level and their way of thinking.

Sales success relies very much on continuity of effort - forming habits and sticking to a modus operandi that has been proved to work. In your role of decision-getter, you have no idea when the YESs are going to appear. They are the peaks in a graph of your effort - but peaks cannot appear without the troughs on either side. So the significant thing is not the number of sales that are created, but the number of people that are constantly being contacted in the process of decision-getting. Performance ratios will change as experience is gained. Prospecting will become more selective by being better qualified, your performance skills in interviewing people will expand and your familiarity with the *Four-Square-Selling* system will add more credibility to your performance.

These are all factors that will add up to one thing - increased sales, and therefore, increased earnings.

# ...and in conclusion...

Selling is something in which we all indulge constantly, every day of our lives.

Everyone lives by selling something. Whether we are professional people, politicians, entertainers, business men and women, shop stewards, clerics, or simply members of the great proletariat honestly labouring in the vineyards, we are all negotiating, dealing, persuading, convincing, assuring, converting, seducing, coaxing, wheedling, bartering, cajoling, in our efforts to influence others and influence events towards the betterment of our, or their daily lives.

Selling, then, is the gentle art of persuading others - and sometimes ourselves - through which reason might dictate need, and logic can often produce want.

Selling goes on in all stratas of society, not just throughout industry and commerce, but in every aspect of sport and entertainment, leisure activity, political life, and, indeed, at every level of domestic and communal life. On the world stage, diplomacy practised between governments is only selling - persuading by the use of logic and reason, using emotive language presented in coded words - the very *body language* of diplomacy - through which one thing can be said whilst another is implied and understood. One country is not going to be told what to do or how to behave by another, but by the use of subtle suggestion through the diplomatic code, ideas and concepts can be put forward - *sold*, in fact - that could literally alter the course of history. *And all that is happening is buying and selling!*

Fascinating, isn't it? Doesn't it make you realise how important selling is to daily life - simply as a conceptual idea?

Everyone enjoys getting their own way in all manner of things. But to impose one's will on others who may be opposed to an idea or suggestion by pulling rank or employing a more dominant personality to steam-roller the other person's opposition, achieves nothing in the long term. Ideas accepted in an atmosphere of resentment have scant value. If the ideas expressed in the general concept of *Four-Square-Selling,* are applied to almost anything in life, everyone's path would be made smoother, if that is, we accept that...

> *...selling is the creation and development of empathy aimed at getting a decision that should result in lasting benefit to both parties.*

Buyer and seller. The roles are interchangeable and the emotions that either role evokes, are much the same - pleasure at having added value or enrichment in some way to someone's daily life. Selling - and buying - is very much related to reward and recognition. Not just in the practical and tangible sense of prize-giving for achievement, but for the sheer personal satisfaction that is its own reward for a job well done - or perhaps, done at long last - or simply for having been motivated to purchase something that may have been long coverted.

I hope you feel this book has been of use to you, whether you are professionally engaged in selling or not. I also hope it may have created a greater awareness of the importance of human relationships - both public, private and business - not just in respect of selling, but in every aspect of our daily lives.

Good selling!

# *Network & Multi-Level Marketing*

**By Allen Carmichael**

This small book first appeared in 1990, under the simple title "Multi-Level Marketing". It was the first British book to be published on the subject.

Reprinted in 1991, it was re-titled because, by that time, the term Network Marketing seemed to be more commonly accepted - although the term *Multi-Level Marketing* perhaps still expresses the business concept more obviously.

The book is intended simply as an introduction to Network Marketing - a concept through which so many people throughout the world have become significantly rich, many becoming millionaires as a result of the development of their businesses. However, that statement is not sufficient to sell the idea of becoming involved in Network Marketing. The book's aim is to explain to the newcomer just what they *must expect to have to do* if they wish to benefit from the glittering prizes so often associated with the business.

This book, with its clear and concise explanations, has been responsible for thousands of people entering the business of Network Marketing, concentrating as it does on the motivational and human aspects needed for successful involvement in a fascinating industry.

Information passed on verbally and often repeated is always in danger of both erosion and distortion, so a book of this nature has great value as a recruiting and motivational tool. The information it contains is always available, never varies, retaining all its initial freshness as each new person reads it. In the development of a successful down-line, it is essential that everyone speaks the same language and develops the same working habits. The book has been adopted by the industry as one of its 'standard' works and many networking operations use it or recommend it to both their new and existing distributors as an aid to building their business efficiently.

**£4.99**

**Please see the order form at the end of this book**

CONCEPT

# The Network Marketing Self-Starter *(2nd edition)*

## By Allen Carmichael

The name Allen Carmichael has become synonymous with Network Marketing. This, his second book on the subject, was written in response to demands for more information from people who had become fascinated by the Network Marketing/MLM concept, after reading his introductory book, *'Network & Multi-Level Marketing'*.

Network Marketing is a business concept requiring, for the success it can bring, a high degree of motivation and commitment from its devotees. The 'Network Marketing Self-Starter' takes, as its starting point, all the aspects covered in Allen Carmichael's first book, and expands them into a training course. The book is packed with useful and practical information.

It includes *The 100 days plan*, described by many as the ultimate guide to networking achievement. The plan is designed to provide, for those prepared to commit themselves completely to its simple formula, all the evidence the reader will ever need to convince him or her that high earnings are not just possible, *they are realistically achievable* - to people who are dedicated to the idea of *achieving the habit of success*...and the book includes a chapter on exactly that.

### £7.50

**Please see the order form at the end of this book**

CONCEPT

# *Believe you can!*

## By Allen Carmichael

This is a book for anyone who wants to change their life, improve their self-image, become more successful and, generally, better their life-style.   It is based on the simple fact that *anyone can achieve anything* - providing they believe strongly enough in the possibility.

It is *never* too late to change or to make adjustments to your personality.  The book explains initially why we are what we are and then leads the reader through a series of exercises designed to uncover personal potential.     This information is then used as the basis for an Action Plan that anyone can put together for themselves to ensure success and achievement in what ever area of change interests them most.

The feed-back the publishers have had endorses the book's strength. It has certainly changed lives!  It has been instrumental in giving new hope to many people injured by the general world economic situation - people made redundant,  people who have lost money,  jobs, businesses. In short, all those who feel they have been short-changed by circumstances, but are prepared to do something positive about getting back their self-esteem and enjoying really living once again. Failure in life is not just falling down,  but rather,  having fallen down,  not having the wit,  guts or determination to get up and start again...

*This is the book for anyone with a real desire to become a success*

**£6.99**

**Please see the order form at the end of this book**
CONCEPT

From experience we know that once a reader has
used the Order Form in this book,
they have no record of our address and telephone number!

So that the book still contains a permanent record,
the information is as follows...

**_CONCEPT_**
**_Publishers & Distributors of the Allen Carmichael books_**

**P.O.Box 614.   POLEGATE .  East Sussex . BN26 5SS  . England**

**Telephone/Fax:  01323 485434**

## ORDER & REGISTRATION FORM (FSS1)

Please supply.........................copies
**NETWORK & MULTI-LEVEL MARKETING** (ISBN 1 873288 01 8) **£4.99**

Please supply .......................copies
**THE NETWORK MARKETING SELF-STARTER** (ISBN 1 873288 09 3) **£7.50**

Please supply .......................copies
**BELIEVE YOU CAN!** (ISBN 1 873288 03 4) **£6.99**

Please supply .......................copies
**FOUR-SQUARE-SELLING** (ISBN 1 873288 04 2) **£7.99**

**U.K. (only)Postage & Packing charges: 1 book = .50p  2 books = .85p
3 books = £1.35  4 books = £1.75**

Cheque/P.O for the sum of....................enclosed, including P&P charge
<u>Please make cheques and postal orders payable to CONCEPT</u>
**Discount prices for bulk orders are available on request**

**TITLE (Mr. Mrs. Miss. Ms)**..............................................................

**FIRST NAMES**................................................................................

**SURNAME**......................................................................................

**ADDRESS**.......................................................................................

.......................................................................................................

**POST CODE**......................**PHONE/FAX**............................/............................

It would be of interest to us if you would answer the following questions:
Where did you buy this book?.................................................................
Are you in Network Marketing?......Which Network?................................

*CONCEPT* Publishers and Distributors of the Allen Carmichael books

P.O.Box 614 . P O L E G A T E . East Sussex . B N 26 5 S S . England
Telephone & Fax: 01323 485434

**NOTE: If you would like to be placed on our mailing list for news of future
publications, please fill in the appropriate part of this form and post to us.**